Other books by
Raymond Strait

Mrs. Howard Hughes
The Tragic, Secret Life of Jayne Mansfield
This for Remembrance (The Rosemary Clooney Story)
Lanza (The Mario Lanza Story)
Star Babies
Lou's on First (Biography of Lou Costello)

HOLLYWOOD'S CHILDREN

RAYMOND STRAIT

ST. MARTIN'S PRESS • NEW YORK

Library of Congress Cataloging in Publication Data

Strait, Raymond.
Hollywood's children.

1. Children of entertainers—United States—Biography.
2. Moving-picture industry—California—Hollywood.
I. Title.
PN2285.S74   791.43′028′0922 [B]   81-23180
ISBN 0-312-38837-3   AACR2

Design by Laura Hammond
10 9 8 7 6 5 4 3 2 1
First Edition

For Kenneth Norris who has, through the years, been the loyal friend everybody hopes for but rarely ever finds.

and

For my daughter Shaunna who will not shut up until she sees her name in print. (I love you, sweetheart.)

Contents

☆
☆
☆

Acknowledg- ments

Nonfiction books require a tremendous amount of re- search and cooperation from sources about which the reader seldom if ever knows. This book was made possible not only by the cooperation and kindness of the children who are the subjects, but by numerous others who, by word of mouth, passed me along from one of Hollywood's children to another. To them and to others who lent a hand in helping me locate some of these celebrity off- spring, I want to express my thanks:

Paul Blane, Dr. Terry Robinson, Chris Costello, Ken Norris, Leo Guild, Mrs. Jackie Cooper, Mamie Van Doren, Buck Buchanan, Richard Clark and Jim Waggoner of American Management, Inc., Keenan Wynn, Wendy Maree, Debby Katt, and Kirk Crivello.

A very special thanks to Dominick Abel, the best agent any writer ever had, for his confidence and guidance; my appreciation of Tom Dunne, Pam Dorman, and Ashton Applewhite (my editors at St. Martin's who understood me and knew how to cut away the verbiage without damaging my ego); and John Murphy who, better than anybody, knows how to publicize a book.

Foreword

Being a celebrity, constantly in the public eye, is difficult. Being the child of such an individual is often an impossible task. As one of Hollywood's children explained, "How can we possibly be normal or know who we are when our parents don't even know who *they* are."

Youngsters come to Hollywood looking for stardom, fame, and fortune. What they find is a hard-nosed business whose only interest in you is how marketable you are as a commodity. First their names are changed to Lola or Brett or something equally alien in order to fit and look good on the theater marquees; and all too often life stories are wiped out and rewritten by a publicist, agent, or studio head.

These people then marry (today they may not) and have children who grow up in the celebrity ghetto with a false identity, false sense of values, and very little, if any, sense of normalcy as most who read this would understand.

Here, then, are the *real* autobiographies of the off-spring of celebrities, told in their own words. They have revealed frustrations, rejection by parents, tremendous love for parents, being loved by parents (often surrogate parents), ambitions, and the glitter world they were tossed into as one said, "simply because we are the by-products of fame."

Mommie Dearest was one child's ordeal. These accounts represent an entire community. One cannot read this book without resultant mixed emotions because there is no stereotype—no *typical* celebrity sibling.

Raymond Strait

Three generations of show business pose for a family portrait: Tracy Keenan Wynn, now a prominent television and motion picture screenwriter; his father, actor Keenan Wynn; Keenan's father, the great comedian Ed Wynn; and Ned Wynn, also a writer and Keenan's oldest son.

Courtesy of David Kovar

1

☆

☆

Tracy Keenan Wynn

Keenan's son Tracy is brilliant—almost bitterly brilliant. When I interviewed him at the Beverly Wilshire Hotel in Beverly Hills he was in town on business for only a few days. Home these days is Aspen, Colorado—far from the Hollywood he grew up in and (once) seems to have loved. I think he loves his work as a screenwriter but hates what Hollywood has become since he moved away. To me he seemed a young man trying hard to appear serene, while a storm of protest and discontent was raging within.

Polite, well-mannered, and a good conversationalist, I had early on decided that the interview would be just as he had predicted—*dull*. It was only afterward—once the tapes had been transcribed and Tracy had added a few notes—that I realized Tracy Keenan Wynn is anything but "dull." The seeds of controversy seem to have been sown during his teen years as he grew up in the "dope generation" and hated everything for which it stood. As an adult, his film works have all been about social issues—with strong middle America mores.

He is a young man who possesses the qualities of leadership—and I'm sure he will take his "Hollywood" upbringing and use it to become a strong voice in the film industry.

As a fourth-generation show business arrival I have, without a doubt, a whole lot to live up to: Frank Keenan (my great-grandfather), the celebrated Shakespearean actor and Broadway matinee idol; Ed Wynn (my grandfather), a star of stage, radio, films, and television—but surely more remembered as a clown, who for years spoofed himself as "The Perfect Fool"; Keenan Wynn (my father) has appeared in nearly three hundred films and continues to amaze me with his abilities as a dramatic actor. These are heavy acts to follow. But, what the hell . . .

In 1945, my father inadvertently upstaged me—for the first and only time. Mother was riding home from the hospital in an ambulance with her newborn son bundled in baby blue bunting—little ol' me. We were heading west on Sunset Boulevard, when another ambulance passed us, traveling in the opposite direction, with sirens screaming and red lights flashing. It was en route to the emergency room with Dad, who had just been in a terrible motorcycle accident and was in critical condition. Ironically, he had been on his way to the same hospital to escort his wife and heir home when it happened.

Many things affected me as a child, but nothing that brought on any great traumas. I was too young to remember when Mother divorced Dad and married Van Johnson. She was granted custody of me and my older brother Ned. In 1948 Mother and Van had their own child together—a daughter, Schuyler, so I grew up in a home with three children. Dad later remarried—to Sharley, a great lady—and it's lasted twenty-eight years. Hallelujah! They have three daughters, Hilda, Wynnie, and Emily. The family tree sort of looks like it was struck by lightning.

My earliest real memories are of Van and Mother. I was about four, I think, when I began to understand any of what was going on. When I was young, I often visited my father, but I never had any identity crisis as far as who my parents were. Van was "Van," Sharley was "Sharl," and Dad and Mom were just that. I was, by nature of my living conditions, closer to Van at that time in my life. But Dad made the best of a difficult situation and was careful to keep a very close relationship with Ned and me. He saw us on weekends, and in the summer we'd go on camping trips together. In order to have special times with both of us, Dad would sometimes have a weekend with each of us alone—time he shared individually with his sons. In a way, the separations brought Dad and me closer—a good relationship that continues to this day.

Those early years meant lots of fantastic weekends for me. Car races. San Francisco. Movies. Dad was still under contract at MGM where he stayed until about 1956. On Saturday mornings he used to take me over to the studio where a sympathetic projectionist would run all the latest *Tom and Jerry* cartoons for us. We had our own private picture show—and it was great. Once there was a birthday party for Judy Garland. I can't remember exactly when this was, but she was *the* superstar, so they really rolled out the royal purple trappings. They even had Leo the Lion show up. There were always plenty of status-oriented birthday parties. I won't bore you with the details because they were all the same bullshit and you'll probably hear all about it from somebody else. At any rate, we all went— more for the parents, I suppose, than the kids.

Hollywood was undergoing tremendous changes during the early fifties. The impact of television had a lot to do with that. Also, Europe was becoming more and more a movie center, which didn't actually peak until the late fifties. Van took advantage of that and we moved to Switzerland and England for a time. More and more films were being shot on location and away from the studios. Van's pictures were mostly musicals or "big pictures," while Dad continued as a major charactor actor—when you could get him off his motorcycle! From his early days at MGM Dad was into motorcycles—even before they became fashionable. He rode with Clark Gable and Ward Bond and only quit riding when we took his bike away at age sixty! Louis B. Mayer, the *real* Leo the Lion of MGM, once got onto them all about their haphazard and dangerous away-from-the studio activities. You couldn't blame him. All that expensive talent taking all those chances. I hate motorcycles myself. I've never been on one—and never will, either.

Celebrity families changed, right along with Hollywood. My home life was comfortable. By some standards, perhaps even sheltered. We were all pampered to an extent, of course. It was Hollywood, after all. There was no harshness about my home life—none of the Joan Crawford syndrome. Nevertheless, there were parental guidelines. Just limits that we knew, understood, and respected.

My mother was the family disciplinarian, but when spankings were called for she sent us to Dad. Actually, I don't think I really did anything too terrible, except once, when I was about ten. I burned down part of the guesthouse. I was playing with matches and I set fire to the outside staircase. Interestingly enough, Dad did not punish me that time. Oh, he talked to me about it, of course, but man-to-man. In a way, I remember that talk a lot better than I do the spankings.

I grew up quite close to my mother. We had our differences and frictions, but nothing that isn't normal in any mother/son relationship. There was never any giant schism, and Van was a decent and good stepfather. We always got along. Our family is probably the supreme example of Beverly Hills/entertainment world marriage, divorce, and remarriage. Everyone got along remarkably well in spite of the complicated genealogy, although finding out who is what took time.

Ned and I were close as youngsters, but as we've grown older, we seem to have grown apart. Actually, our times and friends were different. He's four years older than I; when I got to high school he was in college. When I was at UCLA he was meditating with the Maharishi in India. While I was still studying film technique to stay out of the Vietnam War, Ned was into producing rock 'n' roll records with Doris Day's son Terry Melcher. I was never really a part of the meditation scene. I find most of it very irritating. All of those self-awareness programs and cults are supposed to help you know yourself, but I think they're really just a scam to make money. Ned and I could never agree on the worth of meditation.

Perhaps my own comprehension of our family situation precluded my becoming interested in finding myself outside that arena. Having always been family oriented, I sought close family ties. I didn't want to fall into the situation my father and grandfather had. There was always some friction between them from the time Dad was seventeen until he was thirty-one; that's a long time not to have an honest dialogue with one's father. Ed had a very difficult time accepting the fact that Keenan was a dramatic actor instead of a clown like him. Looking back, it might seem a small thing to fester into a family quarrel, but it was real enough to them. I've really tried to stay close to my parents—and grandparents—and to overlook whatever differences we have. Sometimes it actually works!

I remember my grandfather Ed with great fondness. We played backgammon together from the time I was twelve years old until I was twenty-one. Toward the end of his life Grandpa and I were quite close—the last three or four years particularly. I think I was as close to him as Dad was, maybe even closer. Ours was a very contemporary relationship. Ed was a vigorous man right up to the end, when he suddenly fell victim to throat cancer. He endured a tremendous amount of pain near the end and he finally started to lose weight and age very fast. One time Grandpa and I were in the elevator riding up to his penthouse apartment. When an old couple got on and rode up part way with us, Ed studied them in silence. After they got off and the door closed, Grandpa turned and looked at me. "I don't look that old do I?" he asked. In fact, he did.

"Hell, no! You look like you could be the guy's son." He laughed, but he didn't answer me. He needed some reassurance that he was still the Ed Wynn we remember. In spite of our tremendous age difference, I believe I understood him quite well. Maybe it's because there really is a skip in generations; grandfather and grandson trying to relate to the link in the middle. A common goal. It's a pity Grandpa isn't still here. There's a lot of things that I'd like to talk about with him.

As a youngster most of my friends were the children of film industry people. Everybody and anybody on a predetermined scale of importance. It's standard procedure—status determined by the parents' importance in Hollywood.

I was never interested in being social in the Hollywood sense during my youth. I went to all the usual parties because that was expected—but I never really got off on it. For my parents it was different, of course. That was another era. It was almost a requirement that one go places and be seen. I believe Hollywood is different now. Or at least I hope so. Many of the top film-makers today are more inclined to deal with the nuts and bolts of moviemaking than to worry about social columns. There are exceptions, of course, but this has *got* to be a step in the right direction.

There is another side to all of this business of growing up in Hollywood. Before my time, stars never admitted they had children. It was bad for their image. Bad for the glamour. I was part of that first generation who helped plant the image of Hollywood as a family town before the moviegoing public. Actors were human, after all!

I also grew up in an age of transition, when Hollywood, as well as the country, was going through a great metamorphosis. The international leaders of World War II were gone and the day of the movie mogul was coming to an end in Hollywood. The one-man operation died a slow death. I grew up during this postwar period, which was also the beginning of the struggle of the independent film-makers and small companies to establish themselves. Unfortunately we now have huge corporations trying to run the show. Today film-making is an adjunct to big business. I'm not sure we've grown all that much. I do know, however, that fewer films are being made than were in production during my growing years. Maybe we need moguls again.

Hollywood went through an identity crisis during the sixties. So did everybody. We all were learning difficult lessons as we grew—and usually the hard way. Academics was the biggest disappointment for me. I really thought it was a waste of time. In the sixties, my God! What can I say? Everybody was doing everything. I had a different set of friends and was living a different lifestyle from the one I had at home—sharing apartments with friends and all that. My hair at one time was down to my shoulders. Big deal. Everybody was doing it. But still, when I look at those photos . . .

Tracy Keenan Wynn ☆ 7

Everybody was doing drugs, too—but that's one thing I've really gotten to hate. The whole lifestyle. I hate it with a passion. Today I have friends who say to me, "Gee, you live in Aspen and you don't do cocaine?" They think I'm lying or crazy. I've known a lot of people who have had terrible problems with drugs. To me it was never worth it. Let's put it this way: I've never seen anyone function well creatively under the influence of drugs. That so-called stream of consciousness just led to confused, unstructured anarchistic crap. I've seen actors' performances ruined by booze and drugs. It's got to be a dead end in the creative sense, especially over a long period of time. I know this firsthand—I grew up in the "drug generation."

Sure, I've gone to some parties and smoked a little dope when I still believed all the drug culture propaganda. But when friends started getting more and more stoned-out and made less and less sense, I knew it was time to split. Pretty soon people were getting into heavier stuff and their personalities seemed to change. When I moved to Aspen from Los Angeles people were chipping cocaine at parties and I could see it was getting to be impossible. Where else do you go? Heroin? Still, there are those starry-eyed wonders who insist that a little pot is OK. Hare Krishna, baby. Drugs, alcohol—I've seen too much abuse to have anything nice to say about them. Recently the young son of a superstar accidentally OD'd on booze and Valium. I have a friend who's become an alcoholic—and has been since school days in Switzerland. I hear he's tried to kill himself. Perhaps I tend to intellectualize and sit on a cloud observing all of this, but I really get irritated, having seen so much grief from drugs and alcohol, when people try and tell me how great dope is. It's a shocker. My father's generation had heart attacks; my generation, all too often, expire from dope.

Peer pressure was something I always ran away

from—with mixed success. Peer-group pressure isn't limited to one's close circle of friends. It is so all-pervasive, in everything from advertising to political chic, that it's hard to avoid. I remember how most of us tried to be so cool that we probably missed out on a lot of things. It's almost the same as joining a fraternity or a club—except none of us would ever admit to such middle-class endeavors. Even the Black Panthers found easy money from some of us, especially one girl who tagged her superstar father for ten thousand dollars. I never saw much difference from ladies in hair-rollers bowling and those people up in the hills doing dope and talking revolution. The revolution, of course, was always something they considered themselves an honest part of. The antithesis and synthesis crowd. There are still a few of these fools around.

Many people my age seem so damned weak, and the reason they're weak is that they've been very lazy, very nihilistic, and very indulged. I guess we all are to an extent, especially in Hollywood, U.S.A, but the true fight isn't political awareness, it's self-awareness—and not self-awareness through drugs or some popular guru or chant.

My parents did a pretty good job, considering the environment. They were wise in not being too structured with us because kids react against too much structure. We were given choices. I'm sure they hoped we had enough background or at least enough smarts to make the right choices. One thing I resented, and still have a bad feeling about, is being sent to military school. Ned went to Harvard School out in the San Fernando Valley and I went to Black Fox Military Academy. I hated the place. In third grade I went to school from seven-thirty in the morning until five-thirty in the afternoon. They made us march—all that unnecessary crap. I would never do that to my kid—ever—unless it was his specific choice. Also, I had to take piano lessons for seven years and today I can't play a note.

I can't read music—I never had an acumen for music—at least not the piano. I would much rather have learned how to box or speak Spanish. But piano was what all the Hollywood parents were into. Piano lessons and military schools. I was in my teens before I realized that all of those things were status symbols. I hope I'm strong enough to avoid pressuring my son into something he isn't meant to do or like.

I really enjoyed living in California in the fifties. But enjoyed it less in the sixties. Now it has gotten so big, even the intersections have become smoggy. I recall when driving out to Palm Springs was a big deal and one could still see snowcapped mountains from Beverly Hills. Now there is usually a yellow hue to everything and it is too crowded and too explosive on Rodeo Drive. I don't really know anybody anyway. It's a bad joke. I go down the streets of Beverly Hills and don't recognize a soul. I used to know everybody on the streets and in the shops. No more. And if you don't have a brown Mercedes, you might as well slit your wrists because the parking attendant won't even consider parking your car in front of the restaurant—a fate worse than not having a face-lift.

I remember being a student at Bel Air Town and Country School—a wonderful school (which is now John Thomas Dye School). That was a uniform school like Black Fox, but I didn't mind wearing the uniform because it was so laid back. More like a family. Small and wonderful. I went to Le Rose in Gstaad after that, so I have had my share of structured schooling. But it was great speaking French and meeting all those incredible jet-setters. Meeting them, but not necessarily liking them.

I started going to 20th Century-Fox on a sort of semi-professional level. I was about eighteen—or maybe younger, because when I was in high school in Europe I'd come back in the summer and work as a go-fer at KABC

Studios. At Fox, I'd watch the shooting and take part in all the different aspects of pre- and postproduction things going on. I never really cared about acting, but I've always enjoyed talking with actors, not *stars*. There's a huge difference. Any good director will tell you!

I appreciate watching good actors at work. As for stars, I was never that interested in what they do outside the studio. Consequently, I've never been starstruck in the usual sense. There are people in the industry I admire, but I have no screen idols.

Contrary to my heritage and what people might expect, my family had no influence at all in my becoming a screenwriter. I'm the first college graduate in our family. My father didn't even go through high school. So writing was never a thing in our family. Frank Keenan was a Shakespearean actor, Ed was a vaudevillian, radio star, and later television and film actor. A clown you could call him. And Keenan has always been a dramatic actor in films. Naturally, I thought I wanted to be an actor when I was very young. I would see films and say, "Ah, I can do that." But when I got older I knew that profession was not for me. Acting is a craft for which I have no facility. It makes me uncomfortable. I did get my feet wet as a movie actor, however. I was in *What's New Pussycat?* as a psycho and did some dubbing in French over in Paris. I felt awkward and knew I had to find something else.

After graduating from the UCLA Film School, I joined the junior training program at 20th Century-Fox Studios. I was into that for three years. I was paid one hundred dollars a week along with five others. We were kind of go-fers for everybody. But more importantly, we could observe. I was involved with quite a few segments of the television series *Voyage to the Bottom of the Sea.* I'd be there at five-thirty in the morning. It was like being a third assistant director. Then I was in the editing department for a while. I wasn't allowed to touch the film, but I watched the dailies with great interest and saw a number of films put together. I was starting to move up in production when I met a gentleman named Marvin Schwartz and told him about an idea I had. He said, "Why don't you write it down?"

I discovered I really liked writing it down, so I expanded and expanded—and the story became *Tribes*. *Tribes* went on to become a television movie and we won an Emmy for it.

I had done a couple of television things with Grandpa. We did the first New York–Los Angeles live feed show and there were a lot of premieres and studio functions—and being with Van (who was a superstar at the time), we used to travel in high style—all through Europe in limos and crossing the Atlantic on the *Queen Elizabeth* and meeting Lord and Lady "Whoozit"—it was an obvious celebrity situation. All that changed, in the course of events, as new actors took the spotlight away. But life goes on. Dad never got hung up on the celebrity kick (nor did Ned and I). He was more of a trendsetter.

Writing, like acting, is a craft. In that respect, Dad and I have a professional quirk in common. I think when you hang around something long enough you will pick up on it by osmosis if nothing else. I never thought of being in any other industry. I never wanted to be an airline pilot, soldier, policeman, fireman, or even the president, for all that matters. If I hadn't gotten into screenwriting, I'm sure I'd be doing something in film-making, although I have no idea what that something would be.

As you might surmise, growing up in Hollywood for me is viewed in retrospect through perhaps a different lens than most of my contemporaries. I think that's because I always maintained my own individuality and didn't succumb to the all-too-present temptations to fall in line with the rest of the crowd. Basically, I'm satisfied with my up-bringing. If I could change anything it would probably be to make us a little closer as a family—I'm sure you'll hear that plea from many Hollywood kids who have grown up under the system. The closeness was not there as much as it should have been, perhaps, but at least it was there. I don't know about *normal* upbringings—how close *normal* people are to their parents—but I have no regrets. I don't think what I've experienced is so very far removed from what most young adults might say about their own parents. At least I haven't met anyone yet who told me their parents were *perfect*.

I would like to have made a million dollars by the time I was twenty and I didn't. Darn. It would have been nice, but it is not something that's going to drive me to drink. I'm happy with the way things have gone for me. One thing I might comment on—I was always aware of who I was and who my parents were. I knew I was a celebrity child—one of Hollywood's Children.

Suzanne LaCock mugs it up with her famous father, Peter Marshall.
Courtesy of Peter Marshall

2

Suzanne LaCock

Peter Marshall's daughter Suzanne is a free spirit, a product of the campus unrest that cast such a pall over the country during the sixties. She is nothing like the era she emerged from at the end of her student years. She might have been a "Pretty Girl" pinup in gingham or pinafores. She is the girl next door with brains.

She readily admitted that there had been friction between her famous father and herself, but no more so than her siblings have. Peter Marshall, she says, does not think of himself as a rich man—and never has—which created resentments on her part when she went away to college. Those resentments, thanks to therapy, have dissolved. She is now in the "business" herself as an associate director on a network television series, which has brought about a greater understanding of her father, she says, and fulfillment to her own life. Suzanne is an All-American beauty and a truly liberated young woman.

I suspect that the most important aspect of this interview is the relationship between my father and myself. I can talk about what my life was like growing up with a struggling actor, whereas my younger brothers and sisters can tell you what it is like to grow up with a celebrity. I was the oldest and the one who most resembled my father, both physically and emotionally. In my earliest and most formative years my father was rarely at home because his work forced him to be away for months at a time. By the time *Hollywood Squares* came along for him, I was on my way out of the nest. The only time that I can clearly recall anything that resembled a "normal" childhood was when we lived in England and Dad was appearing in *Bye Bye Birdie*. For this reason, and because I truly loved the people and the life of London, I still remember that time as being the happiest of my childhood. It gave me a thirst for travel to other lands to learn new customs and meet people of other cultures. This has proved to be a motivating force in my life.

I have an uncanny memory. I can remember being in the crib in my room. I recall living in Van Nuys, California in an apartment with my mother and being bored.

I was bored because I had no one to really play with or talk to. I have always preferred adult company. I never really enjoyed being a child or playing with other children. I would rather sit in a room with my parents' friends and listen to all their fascinating and funny stories. I can't recall anyone ever being around who wasn't somehow involved in the business of entertainment. They always seemed so witty, clever, and talented. I wanted to be exactly like them and when I grew up I wanted my friends to be like them as well. Today, most of my friends are in fact related to the industry in one way or another.

I only experienced such boredom for the first three years of my life. After that my brother, Ralph Pierre (Peter) LaCock II, was born and neither I nor any other member of my family would ever be bored again.

From the beginning, I went to a number of different schools. We would sometimes follow my father around, but soon the family grew too large to make that practical. My father is successful now, but he wasn't constantly working while I was growing up. He was an actor, singer, and a straight man in a comedy team (Noonan and Marshall; later Marshall and Farrell). He wasn't a star. I was moving out of the house just as he was becoming a household name.

There were the moments of success, for example, when we were in England, but Dad's real forte was the stage. In California, it doesn't matter if you're a Broadway star because nobody is going to know anything about you. Movie and television stars have the fame. Dad was neither of those things. When people asked what my father did for a living and I'd say he was an actor, they simply did not believe me. He wasn't in the movies or on television every week. I remember when my aunt Joanne (Joanne Dru), Dad's sister, was starring in a television series called *Guestward Ho* and I could say, "Well, my aunt's a star." I took every advantage of that piece of notoriety. Kids identify with whatever is current. Aunt Joanne had also been a tremendously popular film actress, but my peers didn't remember that.

In some ways my father and I have a very close relationship and in others quite distant. I grew up without a normal home situation. My friends' fathers who were not in show business left home at nine in the morning and returned at five in the afternoon. My father often left in June and I wouldn't see him again until October when he was out of work. I always knew when he was unemployed because that's when he was home. I sensed the strain in the house whenever he was home. I never doubted that my parents loved each other or us, but it was quite apparent that they were constantly struggling to make ends meet. In the early years they didn't have the luxury to analyze or assess their relationship. When Dad did come into his own after twenty-some years of marriage—and was finally able to live at home full time—he and Mom were in some respects like strangers. All the kids were grown and it seemed like my parents should have been able to sit back and relax together, without financial worries. But it wasn't to be. They tried for three years to get back to where they were when they started out, but it was too late. They had grown in different directions and no longer had the common interest upon which their love had originally been founded. They agreed to a divorce.

Mom had always been more "mother" than Mrs. Peter Marshall. She never cared to share the spotlight with Dad. I can't vouch for her feelings, but it was traumatic for me not to have my father around. It is different today when so many kids are from single-parent families. Even though Mom and Dad were married, they were separated so much of the time that basically I grew up with one parent. I never had the feeling that my father was deserting me, at least in my early years. Later, when I became a teen-ager, I relished his being away from home because he was so strict when he was there. My whole social life would come to a screeching halt the minute he walked through the front door. He would put my dates through such an old-fashioned interrogation it was embarrassing. Even when I came home to visit, after being out of the house for ten years, he imposed a midnight curfew on me.

I believe that happens to the eldest child, no matter what. I was caught up in breaking the barriers for the children coming up behind me. Jaime, my younger sister, for instance, moved out of the house to live with her boyfriend when she was seventeen and no one even batted an eyelash. When I pierced my ears at the same age, I was grounded for months. To some degree there was a double standard between the sexes in our home. Even so, whenever we went out with visitors, male or female, Dad would still wait up until we were safely home for the night. He had traditional roots and maintained certain standards.

With regard to my brothers and Jaime, I'd like to explain their effect on my life: First there is Peter, the second eldest—my first sibling and brother. Peter, the athlete (now a Major League baseball star). For years we did not get along at all. I often told him, "If you ever have a son, I hope he's exactly like you, so you'll know what it's like to be driven crazy!" (He has two daughters!) He was the type of boy, if you just touched him on the shoulder at six o'clock in the morning he'd bounce out of bed all smiles, cheerful, and singing, ready to beam sunshine on the world. At Christmas I'd practically beg him, "Please, Peter, let's open the presents after lunch." I've never been one who functioned well early in the morning. Peter would be the first one up and had all the presents opened when the rest of the family awakened. Same thing on Easter. The rest of us would get up at a normal hour only to find that Peter had found all the eggs, eaten all the candy, and was looking very much like the cat with canary feathers in its whiskers.

Yes, he was the "thorn in my side" as I was growing up. He was full of all kinds of ideas to drive me crazy and more often than not he succeeded. But I was also the first one he came to with a problem. He was the kindest and the most sensitive when it came to caring for animals (he still is) and he was always protective of me. Today (as I'm taking off to see him play baseball in Japan) I see him as the most stable and financially secure of our group. He is a responsible family man, devoted and loving father and husband. He is in his own right a "celebrity" and because

Suzanne LaCock ☆ 19

his name, LaCock, is always recognized I now rarely have trouble cashing a check. People are always nicer to me when they make the correlation between myself and my brother.

My brother David was quite different. He never had Peter's aggression and competitive spirit. Like the rest of us, he is the same person basically that he was as a child. He was the dreamer, the naked boy singing in the flower beds. He's not made for the life here. He lived in a tree in Hawaii for years, has married and sired a son, Yogi, and was last seen in Bali on his way to India. The movement that started in the sixties still lives with David and I suspect it always will.

Peter and David are only a year apart and although total opposites, they have always been extremely close. Our home was rather isolated at times, so there weren't that many children to play with. Consequently, we usually created our own social life, which resulted in a close-knit family in spite of sibling squabbles.

Jaime, the baby—the most spoiled—the most self-sufficient, is ten years younger than I and she already has her own business, a condominium in Mammoth, California, and will always, no matter what, land on her feet. She grew up as the child of a celebrity and doesn't seem to have suffered from any stigma.

Dad was strict, but we found ways of getting around him. I had my own sense of rebellion. I'd cut school and never get caught. I knew how to "fix" school admission slips, kept a small printing press under my bed, and could duplicate every rubber stamp the school used. Still, if my parents told me to be in from a date by ten o'clock, then I was home by ten.

Sex education was also a part of my teen life. There were no admission slips or school stamps to handle that. There were no formulas. I don't think my parents had a lot of advice on the subject as they grew up—or at least not what we have available today. Neither of them grew up with a father. Mom's dad deserted the family nest when she was only two years old. Dad's father died when he was ten. In order to support two daughters and herself, my maternal grandmother was obliged to place the girls in a convent where they were cared for by the sisters while she worked. As a teen-ager I was too embarrassed to discuss sex with my parents, although they both have always maintained a rather open mind on the subject in spite of my father's overly protecting me.

My mother was a very liberated woman, long before it became the fashion. She was never in the entertainment business unless you can call having children entertaining. She was an airline stewardess when she met Dad (and actually received her private pilot's license when she was pregnant with me). She wasn't gung ho about marrying my father, nor did she go into the relationship with children in mind. She would have been just as happy to live with him. Dad was the more traditional partner. He wanted marriage. He even went so far as to tell her he was sterile. He had lived with several women and none of them ever got pregnant, so there was some credence to the tale he told Mom. Sterility or no sterility, Mom used birth control with absolutely every one of us children. So much for precautions. If Dad had been a salesman, I'd probably have twenty-seven brothers and sisters.

Mom turned out to be a great mother in spite of the fact she wanted no part of Boy Scouts or Girl Scouts or the PTA or any of those so-called mother responsibilities. We knew not to become joiners because she wasn't going to participate in that kind of activity. She was terrific in every other way.

Although Dad was gone a lot, as I've said, my mother's sister Phyllis always lived with us and was as much a mother to all of us as any one woman could be. Between Aunt Phyllis and my mother I learned that as a woman I could do anything, including building a house—which is something they have done several times! And I don't mean "oversee."

Our house was the place everybody liked to hang out as I was growing into my teen years and my mother was convinced that all my girl friends were doing "things" and I was the only one who wasn't. She allowed them to smoke cigarettes and they could just hang loose with her. She was always ready to listen to their problems and offer advice. They thought she was simply terrific. She could be very objective when it came to the daughters of other people—so liberal and open. I was not totally included as a part of her liberal attitude toward my friends. Some of my childhood girl friends have children in junior high school and it has always been a joke that I would have babies that their children could baby-sit.

Although there was never any hitting in my family, there was plenty of yelling and screaming. We scream a lot. That's the only way to be heard when we're all together. Many of my friends, however, have remarked that there was more open affection in our home than in their own.

We had six and often seven people in the family at one time and only one bathroom until I was almost a teenager. So it was not unusual for me to take showers with my brothers. We had an openness about our sexuality that *wasn't* sexual. We all still enjoy nudity and to this day nobody thinks anything about it if one of us walks around the house nude. We were never taught any shame about our bodies. I sometimes think that people associate wild and sexually promiscuous behavior with people in the entertainment industry. Oftentimes this view is quite accurate, but fortunately even though it might have been going on I was never exposed to that sort of lifestyle. My mother would openly discuss sex with me and at the same time respect for one's body and self was also stressed. My initial reaction to her descriptions of what constituted sex was probably much like what any eight-year-old's might be. I found the whole thing to be ridiculous and disgusting. With time and experience that image changed. Our parents were always very open physically with each other as well as with us. *I* think that as a result, we all appear to have a very healthy and open attitude with regard to both our sexuality and our bodies.

We were never forced to do well academically at school. My parents always stressed that we should enjoy ourselves and take pride in whatever it was we were doing. We put the pressures on ourselves to excel. Even though I did all the things that were supposed to make one happy in high school (I was a cheerleader and the Prom Queen), I hated it. At Taft High School in Woodland Hills the campus was built to accommodate twenty-five hundred students and when I attended the enrollment was five thousand. I went to school on split days. My first class was at seven in the morning and I was out by eleven. With thirty-minute classes, both the students and teachers were exhausted.

It is very possible that other children of celebrities were closer to the business than I was. I have had a few tries at acting. I went to a theatrical school in England and while I was there I did a few commercials. When I returned to the States I again made an attempt but I was never really too successful. When I was on my own and really working to survive I was able to realize more and more how hard it must have been on my father. Plus, with the way I look I was never really asked to do much more than "jiggle." I hate to be stereotyped as the "dumb blonde"; parts of that caliber were all that were ever offered. So I decided to go into the production end. Fortunately, this has proved to be much more enjoyable and profitable for me.

I'm just beginning to have a sense of success in my life. I always have been terrified of not being successful. I never again want to live like I did in my earlier years. I know that I still maintain a lot of irrational insecurities as a result of those years. I'll overcompensate today for things I didn't have years ago. Little things, like overeating at a party because in the back of my head there's this voice reminding me that there's nothing at home. Or I'll buy every human being I've ever known a gift at Christmas because I never could afford to give anyone anything before.

Actually Christmas was a major contradiction in my childhood. When my parents first told me about Santa Claus, I couldn't understand how any one person could possibly do all that in one night. The only thing that swayed me for a while was that we always had the greatest Christmases. I mean we got everything we asked for and I knew Mom and Dad couldn't possibly afford any of it. My favorite childhood story concerns this very fact. My brother Peter (always a big boy for his age) was becoming the laughing stock of the neighborhood because he still believed in the Easter Bunny. I pleaded with Dad to do something about this. So one evening we all (my father, mother, aunt, and myself) marched into Peter and David's room for the big confession. David took it just fine, but Peter was so distraught he just couldn't believe his ears. When he said, in his shaking little voice, "But there *is* a Santa Claus, right?" Dad, not wanting to further upset him said, "Yes." I had to stand in the doorway, not letting him leave, until he told Peter the whole story. All my brother could say was, "There has to be a Santa Claus; we can't afford it!"

Dad might disagree, but Peter is really very much like him. The one thing he definitely acquired from my mother, however, is his competitive spirit. In many ways I'm the black sheep of the family. I'm the only one who doesn't have that competitive spirit. I'm the nonathlete. At least I'm not when compared to the other family members. I never rush out to play badminton or something equally competitive. Mother never had the attitude, "Oh, this is my child, so I'll give a little advantage." She played every game like it was the final game of the World Series. The whole family plays with a killer instinct—except me.

When I left for college I was very much on my own. Dad did give me some financial assistance, but in the five years I was away at school he only visited once. I'm not complaining because I preferred being left alone. I went to the University of California at Santa Barbara during the late sixties and early seventies. It was a time of change and upheaval with the school systems, the lifestyles, and the country in general. I was actively involved in all of it. I protested the war. I hitchhiked around Europe, Mexico, and Hawaii. I bought all my clothes in thirft shops and I experimented with every available drug. Today my life is somewhat more conservative, but I've maintained a lot of the basic philosophies that I developed during those years. I'm still a vegetarian. I still oppose the Vietnam War (or any war for that matter), and I strongly advocate gun control. I'm actively working to end world hunger. I'm a feminist. I no longer have any curiosity about drugs, but at the same time I don't regret any of my experimentations in that area. I know that I'm not missing anything because I've done it all. I no longer buy my clothes at thrift stores, however, and I still wonder how my parents were able to put up with me during that time. It was a period of tremendous growth and I wouldn't change a thing.

By the time I was out of college I moved to Europe

and it was during this period that my parents were divorcing. It was around the same time that I began to harbor a lot of resentment for my parents. I began to blame them for a lot of the problems I was having. Fortunately, on two different occasions, I've gone into therapy. I've come to realize that, yes, my relationship isn't perfect with my father. We've never been very honest or open with each other. That's partly my fault. I never confronted him or tried to make a conscious attempt at rectifying the situation.

My baby sister, Jaime, of all people, was the first to let him know that, no, things aren't perfect here. Dad, up until recently, has always viewed his relationship with us through rose-colored glasses. But I think, now that the problems have been acknowledged and we're all willing to work at changing things, our relationship will do nothing but show improvement. I readily take my share of responsibility for whatever has contributed to our problems. I detest people who cop out by saying, "I never had this or that so that's why I'm screwed up and that's why you should all feel sorry for me, and take care of me and never expect me to do anything with myself or my life." I find that attitude totally disgusting. We are who we are because that's who we want to be.

My father was never an ogre. He's a terrific guy with certain qualities I love. He has a wonderful sense of humor and he's crazy about babies and animals. These have since become two important qualities that attract me to other men. But because I know this business so well, I sincerely doubt that I would ever become seriously involved with an actor. Besides the basic insecurities that I've already discussed, I also find a real selfishness with most actors I've known. I find selfishness a total bore.

I've seen how acting can create both an emotional and financial insecurity within the family. After being in the business for this short period I can see why Dad still believes that this is probably the last week he'll ever work. There are very few jobs that have this lack of permanence. One rarely knows what they'll be doing or how they'll be doing it three months from now. No matter how successful he's become, I don't think Dad is truly relaxed or assured of his position. Because of this, he's never seen himself as a wealthy man. I think he believes that, sure, I might have some money now, but God knows how long this is going to have to last. People, I think, might assume that I was given whatever I wanted whenever I wanted it. I wasn't deprived of anything really, but I did resent Dad for not helping me as much as I thought he could during various phases of my life. Recently, I'm beginning to thank him for not completely taking care of me and forcing me to do it on my own. Because now I know that no matter what, I can handle on my own just about anything that comes up. And I am secure in the knowledge that if I was ever in any real trouble he'd be there for me.

Mind you, not all of this confidence was always there. I'm in therapy now and I have been for a few years. It helps me to see things more clearly. My brothers, sister, and myself are all quite different, so it leads me to conclude that, yes, your parents do have an effect but they're not the beginning and end of it all. We all have different life experiences and we're all born with different personalities that enable us to cope with and react to the world in our own way.

It was always assumed that with my family and my personality I would definitely be the one to go into the "business." I initially reacted to that by going as far away from the stereotype as possible. I was the first person to go to college in my family. I became a teacher and taught at the American Institute in Italy. Upon my return to the States I quite simply couldn't get a teaching job in the area in which I wanted to live so I gave show business a real try. This time, instead of acting, I worked on the other side of the camera. I started by working with my father on two shows. It was at this time that my perspective of this man who was my father changed. Professionally I've never known anyone quite like him. What I've learned from him, and what I've tried to emulate, is probably one of the main reasons for my success today. No matter how hard I try to fight it, I do work well in the entertainment business. I am happier here and more creative than I would have been as a teacher and I'm secure with the fact that I have something else to fall back on.

I guess if I could change my father's profession I wouldn't. I would have liked it if he could have been home more, but then I was given a lot of opportunities that other children never had. I've traveled more than most and I've met and known some very exciting and wonderful people. I love my work and my friends. By most people's standards I've had a very exciting life so far . . . at least I'm never bored.

Eleanor Powell and Glenn Ford with son Peter Ford on the lawn of their large estate in Beverly Hills. Peter was about four or five at the time.   *Courtesy of Eleanor Powell*

3

☆

Peter Ford

Eleanor Powell was one of the brightest dancing stars ever to emblazon the silver screen. Her MGM musicals are Hollywood classics and collector's items. During the golden thirties and early forties she was a reigning film queen. Then, she met and married a young actor named Glenn Ford who was struggling along in Hollywood trying to make a name for himself. Fans and studio moguls alike were aghast that she would give up stardom to marry an unknown and become a housewife, but she did. It would be 1946 before young Ford would costar with Rita Hayworth in *Gilda* and become a household word.

Glenn and Eleanor's son, Peter, now thirty-seven, is a success in spite of his heritage. He overcame the stigma of being, as he expressed it, a biological "by-product of fame." He also conquered crippling rheumatoid arthritis, which struck while he was in college, after doctors told him to prepare for a lifetime in a wheelchair.

Today he is married to Lynda, a lovely lady he met in

college, and they have a small son. He is the very success-ful head of Blackoak Development Company, his own business, which is concerned with taking old homes and restoring them to classic elegance. His income is in six figures and would be the envy of many "stars."

Peter's young life was traumatic because his parents' views on child rearing were at opposite ends of the spectrum. His father was a strict, no-nonsense man who believed in discipline and hard work in equal quantities. On the other hand, his mother was a loving, liberal, easy-going, overly indulgent parent who used her easy nature as a weapon to compensate for her husband's hard one.

That Peter came out of it all with the sanity he now has is itself a kind of Hollywood miracle. When his parents divorced he was fourteen and his rebellion was both violent and traumatic. For several years he and his father did not speak and the gap between them today is still wide. He remains extremely close to his mother whose love he credits with getting him to adulthood.

This is the first time I've ever really spoken out about my childhood or my parents. I've been chased by tabloids for years and have successfully avoided them. It wasn't that I didn't want to talk about my life; I just wanted it to be in the proper format without a lot of editorial inferences and nuances that distorted what I had to say.

I want to be candid about my upbringing, but there are some things I'd rather not get into—so I won't. I don't want to hurt anybody. I have no axes to grind. But I did have a rather interesting upbringing. As the offspring of two stars, I have been afforded the opportunity to do many, many things. Things that the average person wouldn't want to do—wouldn't even be able to do. There have been innumerable benefits.

It is no secret that I do not get along with my father.

The reasons are not important for the purposes of this interview. What is important is that I be as accurate as possible and let the reader decide what it was like to be the only child of Glenn Ford and Eleanor Powell, two of Hollywood's true superstars.

My childhood had many ups and downs and my first memories are few. My father was very strict whereas Mother was much too liberal. One of the problems in their relationship was that he tended to crack the whip in order to compensate for her great feelings of love. That's part of the problem between us today.

I was born on February 3, 1945, in Beverly Hills. A great many people came to our house who were the superstars of their day. Since my mother had been on Broadway before coming to Hollywood I received a large dose of Eddie Cantors, Sophie Tuckers, and others from the stage. Al Jolson and my mother had dated at one time. I remember being very little and going up to Pickfair where I sat on Mary Pickford's knee as she told me stories. In her house there was a big room with all kinds of animal heads mounted on the walls. I suppose they must have been Douglas Fairbanks's trophies. We lived four doors down from her estate. Johnny Green the composer lived around the corner and Fred Astaire lived up the street. Charlie Chaplin was our next-door neighbor. In fact, one Christmas Eve, Chaplin ran over my German shepherd, and the dog died. I suffered much trauma over that.

Ever since I was small I have always liked and been involved with show business and I feel the business "as it was" is far more pleasant for my memory, as compared to the rat race it is now. I collected autographed pictures of movie stars. Most of them I had met and knew, though some I didn't. It's just a little thing I used to do. I don't do it anymore.

As a young boy I was forever being photographed

with my parents—publicity sessions with movie magazines. It was just exploitation. I was exploited because I was the only child of these two people. It was not because of me for myself. I was nothing. I just happened to be the right sperm with the right seed at the right time. I was the by-product of fame. Consequently the atmosphere surrounding us was tuned in to their status. Growing up in Beverly Hills, I was surrounded by famous names. It was no different for me to have Clark Gable come to the house for dinner than it is now for my son who sees my plumber come to dinner. That was my father's business just as mine is building and construction.

My mother and father were married in October of 1943. She was a major star at the time; he was really new in the industry. After their marriage she quit the business. She did one movie, I believe, sometime in the mid-forties with Esther Williams called *The Duchess of Idaho*. But other than that she was the consummate homemaker. Dad's career really didn't get anywhere until he and Rita Hayworth made *Gilda* in 1946. That was about the time Mom went to London and appeared at the Palladium where she earned the money for a down payment on the house they purchased on Cove Way in Beverly Hills. The house had a history and still does. My parents bought it from Max Steiner who composed and conducted the music for *Gone with the Wind*. They would later sell it to a famous cartoonist. It is now owned by Nancy Sinatra, Jr., and her husband, Hugh Lambert.

Mom and Dad were married sixteen years. When they divorced in 1959 I was fourteen. I suppose it was a pretty good marriage, but I became the focal point for many of their problems. Dad didn't want his only son to grow up and become a spoiled movie star brat. He often went beyond what was necessary to enforce that feeling.

For instance, there were times when my friends wanted me to play and Dad would make me spend the weekend doing chores. There were weekends when I spent the entire time chopping wood. I resented that.

On the other hand, he would see my mother take me to the 31 Flavors or Will Wright's Ice Cream Parlor and stuff me full of six milk shakes to compensate for him. It was a catch-22 situation and very difficult for me. I was a roly-poly, tubby, confused boy because Mother tried to make me happy with sweets, while my father wanted to keep me from being overindulged. It was a game they played and I was caught in the middle. To this day I feel like I'm the father and they're the children.

There are some qualities and talents for which I owe my father a great deal. Instead of allowing me to become frivolous, doing whatever I wanted with my time or giving me cars and money or whatever else was being handed out to Beverly Hills children in those days, he did take an interest in me. He did care because he took the time to be strict. Had he been a little less heavy-handed I would have felt better, but he did *try* to help build my character. He had a workshop, for instance, and he taught me the use of tools. We built furniture together. I remember the two of us building all sorts of things in his workshop. I'm sure that led to the ownership of my own construction company.

But it was from my mother that I learned kindness and love and warmth. At sixty-five she is today still a very young lady. She has, for the most part, led a very sheltered life, always relying on others. She functions for herself, of course, but she came up through a system where everything was done for her. The Hollywood star system. Although my grandmother was not a stage mother per se, she was always there. I don't think Mother signed her own checks until she was forty years old. Stars weren't bothered with such details. Then she married my father who picked up where my grandmother left off.

So there was always my father's strict Canadian "what a father is supposed to expect" attitude poised against the soft, warm New England "homey" character of my mother. It was like the warm and cool air rushing together to form thunder and lightning and I always felt the effects.

My father insisted on certain formalities in our home. For instance, our dinner was served at the big dining room table by servants. Although I was not required to wear a tie at dinner, I was required to dress for dinner—we all were. Dad was also a stickler for cleanliness and would, without fail, check my fingernails at the dinner table. They had to be neat, clean, and the right length.

When my parents divorced it was not just their divorce. It was *my* divorce, too. It was the greatest trauma in my entire life. I loved both my parents and I wanted to live with both of them. Since that was impossible, I chose to live with Mom and my father didn't speak to me for a very long time afterward. We still haven't discussed any resentments he may have had at the time about my decision. I don't know if he would even have wanted me to live with him, but he may have wanted to make that decision for himself, not have it made by a fourteen-year-old boy.

From the day my mother filed for divorce until my father moved out of the house it was like living in a world of silence. Our home might as well have been a sealed tomb for the three of us because nobody talked to anybody else. My father maintained his headquarters on one end of the house, while my mother was down the hall at the other end. And you know whose bedroom was stuck smack dab in the middle—mine. I saw the lawyers come and go—my mother had retained the famous Hollywood divorce lawyer, Jerry Geisler. There were mumbled and whispered conferences, bits and pieces of conversation regarding "the boy" but essentially, it was a no-man's-land for me. In many ways, as much as it hurt, I was relieved when my father finally did move out of the house and the divorce was settled.

Yes, I was agonized and resentful. I was almost eighteen years old before any of it made any sense to me. There has been so much bad water under the bridge that it is still too difficult for my father and I really to get together and talk to each other. Too much strain. It has been over a year since we've spoken at this writing. There's been a couple of brief letters, but . . . maybe . . . perhaps one day when I learn to forgive and he learns to accept—when we are both older—perhaps then things will be nice.

But this is about Peter Ford and not Glenn Ford. I grew up in the Beverly Hills ghetto, with all that that entails, including maids, chauffeurs, vast estates with Olympic-sized swimming pools, and so on. I lived across the street from outrageously wealthy oil people whose son was a friend of mine. He killed himself when he was twenty-two. His parents had always indulged him with everything money could buy—then at twenty-one cut off the Ferraris, seasons of skiing in Switzerland, and all that garbage and expected him suddenly to "be a man" and make it for himself. It was tragic because he wasn't (and hadn't been trained to be) emotionally able to handle life without parental financial indulgences. I, on the other hand, was given very little except a great deal of love from my mother—which was very important. Her love is the key to my own survival.

I've done an incredible number of things in my lifetime. I don't know if there is any way of being the son of two stars and living a perfectly normal life. Coming from an affluent family, and having my mother tell me—ever since I was quite small—that there wasn't anything I couldn't do. Thanks to her I have a great sense of worth about myself and an abundance of self-assuredness. I have always succeeded. Always overcame adversity. I feel that today I'm pretty much together, so both my parents must have done something right. I can't fault my father and say he is a terrible person. He can't be all bad, although there have been many bad times.

The offspring of stars are a certain breed of person. We have different problems, always magnified because of who our parents are. One learns to live like that. What the outside world thinks or says doesn't matter that much. The hurt comes from within the community—the celebrity family itself.

The divorce not only was traumatic for me, but there were also some dramatic changes in the lifestyle with which my mother and I were suddenly left. When they were divorced she received the big house in Beverly Hills, which, at the time, didn't have much value. Today it is up there in the million-dollar bracket. She sold it when it wasn't worth much. She now rents, so she has really nothing. Nothing compared to my father's wealth—or the wealth she could have accumulated had she continued her career instead of abdicating her place as a film queen to become Mrs. Glenn Ford.

At the time of their parting the house was probably worth two hundred thousand dollars, but she had no income. At fourteen, the only child, I wasn't ready to go out to work. So she went to the bank and took out an enormous loan against the house to finance a comeback. She developed an act and played Las Vegas, the Diplomat in

Miami, and the Latin Quarter in New York. Her name still had marquee value and she was making top dollar—twenty-five thousand dollars a week, which, in 1959–60, was big money. That's a one-night stand in the lounge now. But she had no business acumen. She had a tremendous overhead—conductor, four dancers, costumes, arrangements—expenses, expenses, expenses. Everybody wanted to fly first class and no one involved really knew how to manage a business. So there was a negative cash flow. There were zero profits.

I was fourteen years old, living in a twenty-room mansion on about two and one half acres with an Olympic-sized swimming pool. It was an enormous estate with a gardener. Just my mother and me and this monstrous house and we had no money. During the three years she was on the road reviving her career I lived alone with assorted caretaker/baby-sitters. It was a hilarious situation. Mother was making big money, but there was no net gain.

She finally had to sell the house. We were broke. There we were, Eleanor Powell and son eating Hamburger Helper and string beans. I remember the real estate brokers would come and marvel at Eleanor Powell and her vast estate. Very very funny. Mother would spend all day dusting and cleaning our palatial estate because she didn't want to spend the money we needed for a maid because we had to have it for food.

Brokers' appointments were made late in the day. When they showed up with their clients Mother would be out by the pool lounging around like we were in the lap of luxury. It was all a front to help sell the while elephant with which she was saddled. I think my father was paying something like two hundred dollars a month child support.

The effect of all this on me was devastating. Mother was working and barely breaking even, my father was gone, and I was resentful. I knew we didn't have any money. My mother was away working and I had only various women who were selected to look after me in her absence. It was a mistake to leave me without either parent at that time. I needed constant reassurance that everything was OK and I wasn't getting it. My father wasn't speaking to me and my mother, bless her heart, was out there somewhere trying to resurrect a career she had given up for her husband and me, trying to make enough money to support the two of us.

Consequently I went off the deep end. I did all the wrong things and was often in trouble with the police. It could have been far more serious for me had I been caught at *some* of the stuff I was up to. Fortunately I wasn't. I'm happy today that those teen-aged shenanigans are buried with my childhood. I refused to go to school, would slip out at night to meet and travel with my hoodlum friends. How I escaped drugs I'll never know. The most I ever did was a little marijuana and that was only for a brief spell. A vodka and tonic after work is about it for me even now. Although Beverly Hills High School was considered pretty straight when I went there, I managed to find the worst element for friends. I thought I was a pretty bad guy—a tough kid. I was angry. I got into fights, and still have scars on my hands from being knifed. I wanted to get as far away from who I was and where I came from as I possibly could.

I chased after a lot of loose women and was educated very quickly about sex and drugs and what life was all about. I became street-wise in a hurry. I'm sure strings were pulled to keep me out of reform school and that if my parents hadn't been who they were I'd have been sent away.

I've always needed attention. In school I was the class clown. Had to be. Not the brightest person perhaps but I needed attention. I remember once in study hall I ate a moth. It was flying around the room and a kid said, "I'll give you fifty cents if you eat that moth." I ate the moth. I did it to be different. To be special. To be noticed because I was me. All my life I had been known and was brought up to be known as somebody's son. All the hoopla in my life was not for me, but for being the child of famous parents. I hated it.

My life was a series of contrasts. I was either catered to or ignored. I received a small allowance. I was disciplined by one parent, loved by another. A skeptic might say, "How could anybody be complaining when they've had so much?" I can only respond by saying, "What do you do when you're in high school, your father makes in excess of one million dollars a year (which doesn't mean you see any of it), and someone comes up to you and asks, 'What are you going to do when you grow up?'" Does one dare aspire to becoming a butcher or a house painter? When you come from an area like Beverly Hills where everyone is driving around in expensive cars and wearing Gucci shoes, it is very difficult to be counterculture and say, "Gee, I really don't care about those things," because the lifestyle does have an effect on you.

I was raised with a group of very wealthy little boys. Boys flaunted the successes of their fathers, just as they do today. Perhaps that's normal whether you're a movie star's son or not. But some things were positively ridiculous in my world. I'm certain the chances to travel with my father and see the world were a tremendous advantage, but how can some of the stupid indulgences fall into that catchall category?

For instance: When I was three my parents wanted me to learn to swim. Instead of enrolling me at the YMCA for a few dollars a year, they built an expensive Olympic-sized pool in our backyard and hired a private swimming instructor. When I wanted to take tennis lessons nobody said I couldn't or that they couldn't afford it. I was taken down to the Beverly Hills Hotel and Pancho Segora became my tennis coach. In that sense I was spoiled and indulged. You take those things for granted when you've had them all your life. It's a bad habit that's hard to break. I sometimes marvel that I have any sense of normalcy.

In addition to the hoodlums I *chose* as companions, I had friends who were the offspring of other celebrities. Composer Johnny Green's daughter Cathy, Michael Reagan (and he's had his share of hassles because of his famous father who now is president of the United States), Dana Andrews's son Steve, and Art Linkletter's daughter who later committed suicide by walking out a window while on an LSD trip. My closest friend lived next door and was not from a celebrity family. Scott Winters McKomis is still my friend and was best man at my wedding. As I grew older Andy Prine and I became friendly along with Peter Fonda who is still a friend. So I had, as a teenager, an assortment of friends and acquaintances from all walks of life.

Because of my attitude and the crowd I ran around with, I did not do well academically at Beverly High. I was content with a D or C—just so long as I passed the course. I was fairly intelligent but school was not the most important thing in my life. Just before I left Beverly High I had an experience that would help me untangle the mess my emotions were tied up in. There was a big Latin test and I had crib notes written everywhere. On books, my feet, my cuffs, my palms—everywhere. The teacher caught me and of course I denied everything. "I *didn't* cheat," I bleated with the passion of mortally wounded sheep at the slaughter yards.

She said, "You come back in here tomorrow and you'll take the test over—without the visual aids."

That night I crammed like crazy, came in the following day, took the test, and received an A. She took me aside after class and asked, "What happened yesterday, Peter?"

I said, "I really did cheat, but I went home and studied hard last night." That experience had something to do with a change of attitude that was not too far up the road. I realized, "Gee, I can really do this if I try. I don't have to cheat. I don't have to be stupid."

With Mother away and Dad not communicating with me I knew I'd never make any changes as long as I was left to my own devices and companions. Mother was in Las Vegas at the time and I went up to consult with her about where I was and where I was headed. I said, "You've got to get me out of all this mess. I can't deal with it anymore." I was in the middle of a strong anxiety attack, was up-tight, angry, and very hostile toward her. The ultimate result was that I was shipped off to Chadwick, a private school in Rolling Hills near the beach. I imagine she consulted with my father, but I don't know that.

Chadwick was a surfer's school. Everybody had blond hair and was into the Jan and Dean/Beach Boys thing. I entered the school with my ongoing nasty attitude. On the day of my arrival I came on like a prototype of The Fonz— my jelly roll, black shoes with taps on the back—that whole scene. I was an outcast at first sight. Eventually I started to come around. Atmosphere can do wonders to provoke change. Chadwick became the real crossroads in my life. I was one step away from the California Youth Authority. I started to straighten myself out. My grades and social life both took on a new and more promising look. Again, I think the love of my mother, although she wasn't home often, was the instrument of my redemption.

I became interested in other things. Once I was able to stop feeling hurt and put behind me the pain and anxiety I suffered from my parents' divorce, I began to look outward and saw other things in life to do and to be a part of. As a teen-ager, I once had my own singing group which we called Peter Ford and the Creations. We played some gigs. I remember living on a houseboat while appearing at a club in San Francisco. That was fun. I had a recording contract with Phillips Records and even recorded a Jackie De Shannon song, which was the thing to do at that time. In fact, my producer was Mike Curb who is the current lieutenant governor of California. I remember Mike when he drove an old Cadillac around Hollywood trying to get somewhere in the music world.

Because my parents were both actors, I think it was inevitable that I try my hand at it. I did and found it fun. I was never anything more than mediocre as an actor, but I liked the idea of not being tied down to one thing forever. Doing a film was like having a three-month job and then moving on to the next thing. I've always been a dabbler of sorts and it is easy for me now to equate my construction business with the film industry. It is a business that deals not in careers, but in projects strung out that make a career. I like that.

There were some interesting adventures for me in films and television. Also on the stage. In my life I have been in a legitimate television series (two as a matter of fact), made records, headlined a Broadway show, played the Pasadena Playhouse with Ethel Waters in *Member of the Wedding,* starred in motion pictures, and even played the lead in an X-rated film that, by today's standards, would probably pass the censorship code with a high rating. I did that one for money. I told both my parents about it. My father was not too happy, but Mother didn't make a big thing of it—and it wasn't a big thing.

There has never been anything lukewarm in my relationship with my father. For instance, when I was a regular on his television series, *Cade's County,* he made it a point to work me harder than the others on the show. I had to toe the line. We had a scene once in which he was supposed to throw me a rifle. We rehearsed and he didn't like the way I grabbed the gun. He said, "You're going to miss it and screw up the scene."

I said, "I can see out of the corner of my eye. I'll look up and I'll see the rifle." In rehearsal, it went well. When it came time to shoot the scene he threw the damned rifle so hard it more than took me by surprise. I'm convinced he wanted me to miss it—to hit me in the face—just to prove that I was wrong because I didn't do it *his* way. But I caught it. It was just another of his unending tests that I'd been put to all my life.

Dad has been married a couple of times since my mother and has also dated a number of nice ladies. I got along very well with most of them. Debbie Reynolds, Hope Lange, Eva Gabor, Judy Garland, and Connie Stevens to drop a few names. I had a big crush on Connie. In fact, one of the traumas of my life involved her. I met her at my father's house and we played pool together. At that time I didn't know it was polite to let a lady win and I beat her for a quarter. I took that quarter home and put it in a special place in my desk. My mother accidentally picked it up and mixed it with other money and I was devastated.

Peter Fonda and I were very close at one point in our young lives, though I don't see him so often now. I one time dated a girl named Ruth Brewer. Her sister Susan married Peter. Ruth and Susan's stepfather is Noah Dietrich who was once Howard Hughes's right-hand man. I remember being up at the Dietrich mansion one day and Noah had a shotgun laying over his knee, teasing me. He said, "If you don't marry my daughter, Peter, I'm gonna kill you."

I said, "Well, Noah . . ." and everybody laughed. Ruth and I did date for five years, but I don't know if we would have ever gotten married—to each other. Might have.

Peter is a free spirit, let us say. At a film festival in Yugoslavia the two of us had an interesting experience. I'm not going to get into the whole story, but I remember us going to the American ambassador's residence and Peter wearing his holster and gun and the American flag wrapped around him. Oh God, it was just too much. He had on all those medals, which were attached to a Confederate uniform and there was a little American flag pinned to his hat. It was truthfully a scene from the sixties set in the wrong country. Luckily we weren't thrown into a Communist jail.

Reaching my late teens, I went to live with my father for a while. We made peace and I accompanied him on a trip to Europe. It was 1964 and we met the Beatles in Stockholm when they were first coming through, which was a big thrill for me. At any rate we were there and I thought, well, we'll try to amend this thing and we did.

This is the other extreme I was talking about. He was single at the time and we really lived it up in Scandinavia. It was great for both of us. We'd pick up girls and double-date and other things. I almost missed a plane once because of those "other things." It was wonderful. We did things that fathers and sons should do.

I graduated high school, of course, and went on to USC. I hadn't been there too long when I received a phone call one evening from George Montgomery. He asked, "How would you like to go to South America with Chuck Connors and star in a western?"

If I thought all of that was behind me, I was wrong. I immediately said yes, quit school, and went to South America to be a movie star. My parents couldn't believe it. The film—and that was a long time ago—was *The Proud and the Damned,* which was recently shown on one of our local television late late shows. The whole thing was an impulsive act on my part. Maybe that's being a dabbler or frivolous.

My college life was also interrupted so I could go to Las Vegas with my singing group. While there we were booked to take our act in as a support on the bill with Peter and Gordon (a very popular group) at The Marina in San Diego. I still had my eye on a career in music and it looked as if the cards were all aces. Wrong. At the pinnacle of all that brilliant future my lights went out. I was stricken with acute arthritis. It was so bad I couldn't walk. I left the group to go on with their own plans, came back to Los Angeles, and rented a small apartment in West Hollywood. A doctor diagnosed my condition as acute rheumatoid arthritis.

My condition was painful—excruciating in the mornings. I remember it being summertime and I had to crawl from the bedroom to the bath. One doctor at a local clinic in Los Angeles was blunt: "You better be prepared to be in a wheelchair for the rest of your life."

"No way," I said. "Absolutely no way." It is the stuff of which tabloid headlines are composed: CRIPPLE MAKES COMEBACK. I had used tremendous willpower to escape the clutches of the rebellion that overtook me following my parents' divorce. I would simply have to call on that strength again. And I did. Doctors tried *their* nostrums, including injections of gold. One day I talked to someone who said, "Peter, you've got to purge your system." That would be some task. In Las Vegas, prior to my illness, I would stay up until four in the morning. It was always partytime with lots of women, late hours, and a hard running life.

All that changed. I stopped eating all red meat, gave up liquor, and started my campaign to stand on my own two feet again—literally. Eventually I was able to stand, then walk with a cane, and finally to run. It hurt like hell, but I would not give up, forcing myself to jog when to do so was agony, but my willpower and faith in my own ability kept me going. Eventually I returned to normal—probably stronger than I'd ever been, thanks to the intense self-discipline and exercise. In addition to walking, I had a new perspective on the value of life.

My mother and father are and have always been religious people. I was not and am not religious. I think it is more difficult for me to be where I am than for those who have their faith in God. They seem to have that wonderful feeling and I envy them. My father, given his own way, would never allow me to feel the way I do. He would argue and say, "You're wrong." If he believes something then I must also believe it.

When my parents divorced I sat down and made a list of one hundred things I'd like to do. I looked over that list a couple of years ago and discovered that I'd accomplished half the things on the list. Many were travel-oriented. One was being a father—and getting married, of course. And this is crazy—I've always wanted to take a kayak all by myself across the channel from Los Angeles to Catalina Island. It's twenty-six miles and strikes me as a great challenge.

In my life I've done so many things. Eaten dinner with presidents, been in jail, graduated from the University of Southern California cum laude, headed up my own realty and construction company where I've bought and sold millions of dollars worth of property, made a lot of money, traveled, married, fathered a son—and but not for certain quirks of fate none of it would ever have happened.

There are tremendous liabilities in being the child of stars. When you are given so much, life becomes uninteresting and boring; it is easy to become jaded. I would much rather not have been born the son of movie stars. I wouldn't ever want my son to be the child of a star. I know people who have children and can't wait to find them an agent so they can get into commercials, on television, or into movies. There's so much loneliness. I can't imagine why anybody would have the ambition to come to Hollywood, become a star, and then subject their children to the life that is forced upon them simply because they are the biological result of a famous person's lovemaking. Stars aren't happy, so how can their children possibly be?

Celebrity unhappiness takes many forms. I've attended a lot of crazy parties with wild things happening—all because of boredom, loneliness, or unhappiness, or all three. At a party given by Joan Blondell the wife of a famous producer seduced me in the bathroom. I'm not going to tell you who it was, but with all her wealth and position she was bored and unhappy—just looking for a different thrill.

If people out there in the hinterlands could know what I know in my heart and mind, they wouldn't get on that Greyhound bus and make their way to Hollywood and Vine to be discovered. They ought to stay where they are, read all that garbage in the movie magazines, and just enjoy Hollywood from afar.

I've built my business without using my celebrity background. *I make a six-figure annual income and it is not for being Glenn Ford's son.* In Hollywood there are stars who are loved and revered and there are those who are less than that. I would think that being the son of Eleanor Powell would be a great benefit to me. Being the son of Glenn Ford—I don't know if that would always be to my advantage. I've heard things said about him in the industry that were not so nice.

Patti takes her first steps (or is she learning to dance?) with the help of loving parents Mr. and Mrs. Johnny Johnston.
Courtesy of Patti Johnston Towers

Eighteen - month - old Patti seems not to be impressed with family photos being shown by her famous parents, movie stars Kathryn Grayson and Johnny Johnston.
Courtesy of Patti Johnston Towers

Kathryn Grayson and young daughter Patti pose in the backyard of their home for publicity purposes.
Courtesy of Patti Johnston Towers

4

Patricia Johnston Towers

Patricia's parents—Kathryn Grayson and Johnny Johnston—were the epitome of Hollywood at its grandest—a marriage made in heaven and dissolved with the help of MGM movie moguls.

She accepts having been raised by her mother alone, but occasionally some of the bitterness over the way the studio manipulated her parents slips through, and you know she'd never want that to happen to her.

She is a fun person. Now married with two children of her own, she still holds many connections to the show business world in which her mother once reigned supreme and still maintains the friendships with Colleen Lanza and Francesca Hilton that began twenty-five years ago when they were all Hollywood's Children.

Patricia lives in the western end of the San Fernando Valley where so many second generations of the Hollywood celebrity world have found peace and quiet away from the frenetic years of their childhood when Hollywood was king; where being a movie star meant always looking glamorous, being sure that Louella or Hedda was informed "first" of any impending marriages, births, or divorces—and no glamorous star would have been caught dead with a "girl next door" image. I liked her—and I think you will, too.

I'm another one of those Hollywood children who was raised by her mother but who has great love and devotion for Daddy. As Kathryn Grayson's daughter, people tend to forget that I had a father, but I did. His name is Johnny Johnston, and at the height of his career in films and recordings, he was one of the better known singers during the forties.

I was born at Saint John's Hospital in Santa Monica— "the hospital of the stars"—and brought up in a very conservative Hollywood milieu. My fondest memories of my childhood are of traditional homey things—nursery school with lots of love and attention and hot chocolate on cold days. Nothing exceptional. My mother was divorced from Dad when I was about two years old and never remarried. She never led a jet-set lifestyle and I truly believe she tried hard to ensure that I had as normal a home as possible. As a movie star, she should have known that "normal" is impossible in Hollywood, so I guess you could call my upbringing "normal for Hollywood."

Being a single parent isn't easy; in Hollywood it is murderous. Often, I would have to miss school to travel with Mother, especially after the death of my grandmother, who had played surrogate mother while Mother was out of town playing club dates.

When grandma died I simply picked up and went with her—and loved every minute of it. Loved the hotels. Loved the room service and even being by the pool—the celebrity life.

There were never any wild parties after the show nor any real night life. Mom was busy at night and slept during the day, which gave me the opportunity to develop a social life of my own—and I always did because I was curious about everything.

When I was a child, movie stars were treated like kings and queens at the big hotels. The penthouses, limousines at their disposal, and always someone at your elbow to do your bidding. It has changed. Too many big names play in Las Vegas to roll out the red carpet every time a star comes to town. It is business and money—no frills.

I spent a great deal of time in dressing rooms and backstage at a very early age and was totally enamored of the show business atmosphere. It was during that period of my life that I developed a great love for the business, despite a rather strict upbringing.

Manners were very high on my mother's list of requirements. I always was given some leeway, but never as much as most of my contemporaries. I often was quite late getting to bed because of Mother's schedule, but those were our times together and so she bent her own rules to accommodate that. We would sit up in bed together late at night having scrambled egg sandwiches with hot chocolate while we watched *Vampira* on the late late show. Mother never sheltered me from anything that even remotely involved me—family problems, debts, illness—even death. Consequently I had to grow up rather quickly—yet, I still had a childhood.

Mom often had premonitions of things to come—and was uncannily accurate. A few weeks before my grandmother's death, I was visiting my cousin Timmy in Encino. Every night, my mom kept having a dream of a little blonde head going down in a whirlpool—and immediately her thoughts went to me. She kept phoning up and bugging Uncle Mike. "Is Patty all right? Are you sure? Can you see her?" Finally he said, "Katie, it is Sunday morning already and if you're so worried why don't you have Paw Paw (my grandfather) come and pick her up because I don't want to hear any more about it. You worry too much." That was at eight-thirty in the morning. Grandpa came and brought me home. At ten o'clock Uncle Mike phoned to say that Timmy had just drowned in the swimming pool. My aunt Julie had heard the splashing but thought he was still playing in the sprinklers. A gardener had left the gate to the pool area open and he ran right into the water and that's where they found him. It was a nightmare—and he had beautiful blond hair.

I learned quite early, therefore, about death. There was Mario Lanza's death—he was like another member of our family—and a whole series of family deaths—and divorces. There are always divorces in Hollywood. In that respect one grows up very quickly. I don't know why it is that stars' homes always seem to draw tragedy—but they do.

My mother cared about people and was always deeply involved in the lives of others. We were very much into ESP in the early fifties, even before that got to be the rage. Mother always knew about reincarnation—so I grew up believing in that. Although my mother is old-fashioned in a lot of ways, she was very much before her time in thinking that it is only natural to assume that we are not the only people in the universe. She was aware of UFO's and used to discuss that with me along with other supernatural phenomena. I am talking about twenty-five years ago!

We had interesting séances, but one has to be careful. It is easy to call on bad spirits if you don't know what you're doing, so Mother and I learned not to mess around with the unknown. We always tried to believe there were only good feelings and good spirits around us. Our friends didn't understand, so we were considered a little weird. There was always the patronizing pat on the back when we'd talk about it and a "Well, there goes Katie with her spirits," condescending attitude.

That wasn't the only reason my friends considered me a little strange. I also happened to like real long-hair music—the classics. My friends who were rushing out to embrace rock 'n' roll just couldn't understand how I could like old music when there were so many new rock artists playing exciting *new* music.

I was my own person from the very beginning—and I was typical in the sense that I idolized my dad even though I only saw him about once every two or three years. When we did get together, it was a big deal in my life. He remarried after the divorce from my mother—four times—and it is very funny—my mother has become very close with most of his ex-wives. Not while they were married, but after the divorces.

Although I didn't see him often, as I say, the times together were great. And let's be perfectly honest. When there's a divorce, there are certain antagonisms. Mom and Dad would talk, but it was an aloof, "Hello, John." Not cold—because Mother is incapable of being cold. Angry and snotty and having fights—all the typical things people do to each other after the divorce—and one baiting another. She baited Dad and he baited her. But you know something? To this day they love each other. If they didn't they wouldn't fight over trivial things the way they still do. They were just incapable of living together and I think I understood that from the beginning. There were executive forces at MGM, however, who were all too willing to encourage the dissolution of their marriage. It was not unusual, I must admit, in those days for studios to arrange both marriages and divorces—even the demise of careers—but that still doesn't make it right.

My father's remarriages had nothing to do with the fact that we didn't see each other often while I was growing up. Not that his wives were against us being together. Not at all. He moved to the East Coast and worked on Broadway and we were living in California—a continent away. A lot of people don't know that my father won a Tony Award for his performance in *A Tree Grows in Brooklyn,* or that he was a contemporary of Bing Crosby, Frank Sinatra, and Dick Haymes—and better looking.

He made one of his films with Mom at MGM—*Till the Clouds Roll By*—and was cut out of the picture by those same forces who were happy to see them break up. I think Dad lost interest in Hollywood after he and Mother divorced—he saw the kind of town it could be and decided it just wasn't what he wanted out of life.

Mom went out on the road after her peak as a movie star. It was the fifties and there was a big change in what the public wanted in film—and what the studios wanted. Musicals were out and she had been typecast as a musical star. That's unfortunate because she is still an elegantly gorgeous woman with a great flair for dramatic acting. But at the time, if you played a singer—just once—in a picture, then you didn't do anything else unless a singing role came up. Such stupidity.

Mom made two or three pictures with Frank Sinatra and when I see those old films I wonder what the kids were screaming about! He was so skinny—not my idea of a sex symbol. Still, the voice was great. It wasn't until the voice and the man matured that I considered him something to scream about. There is a very funny story about Mom and Frank. He really was thin and when it came time for them to have a love scene and the script called for a kiss, she went to Louis B. Mayer and said, "Mr. Mayer, I don't want to create problems, but Mr. Sinatra looks like he might have TB and I don't want to kiss him if he does." Of course, he did not and she *was* kissed! It is funny because millions of young girls would have gladly taken her place—just for the kissing scene.

My dad had the same kind of adulation. While Frank was being mobbed at the Paramount Theater on Times Square, Dad was appearing with Mom up the street at the Capitol—also being mobbed by the milling throngs, having his clothes torn away by screaming teen-aged bobby-soxers—but *he* was handsome. Bob, my husband, was in the audience at one of those shows Mother and Dad did during their 1948 appearance at the Capitol. He was a big fan. Little did any of them know then that the daughter my mother was pregnant with would one day make them his in-laws!

In retrospect, I would have been very unhappy if Mom and Dad had stayed together. I really believe that, now that I'm married with children of my own. I know that they were probably never really meant to be together in the first place. I see them as the prime example of two people who loved each other but are like oil and water. Both gorgeous, talented, beautiful human beings who should never have been married under any circumstances. So their divorce spared me a lifetime of unhappiness.

As I pointed out earlier, I grew accustomed to death at a young age and went to a lot of funerals as a child. Those events took on a greater magnitude because of Mom's attitude. She was never a philosophical person, and while she is strong when she must be, her unhappiness supersedes all. A sensitive person, she is devastated by death—taking everything to heart, just as I do. Her dog died in 1972 and she still hasn't gotten over it.

My mother never tried to be "buddy-buddy" with me, as so many so-called modern mothers try to do today—letting their children call them by first names. Even when I appeared in shows with her we managed to maintain the mother/daughter relationship. My acting and singing flair didn't just happen. In school, I always had the leads in plays—not because I was Kathryn Grayson's daughter, but because I learned from her that performing demanded hard work. I earned the parts I got, and I'm proud of that.

I was ever ready to go out on tour with Mother, but she preferred that I not do that while school was in session unless it was simply unavoidable. My school life was normal, I think. I did well in subjects I liked and not quite so well in those I didn't. I was always good in the artistic things. Music was very important to me. I have an advantage over my mother (and a lot of other operatic singers) in that I sing arias, but I can sing pop, too, and not sound like an opera singer. Mother is a coloratura and I am a lyric soprano—basically the same voice, with that one important difference.

My mother was old-fashioned and I'm a carbon copy in many ways. She was a loving mother but she sure believed in discipline. Morality was always stressed. Mother had the most ladylike image in Hollywood and it wasn't just an image—that's just what she was. The Kathryn Grayson you saw was the Kathryn Grayson you got. There were never any guys under the bed when I grew up—never any hidden pregnancies or any of the things that went on in Hollywood (and were covered up) when I was a child.

Mother dated, of course. I got used to seeing people like Robert Taylor at the foot of the stairs waiting to take her out, but I never saw anyone cross the line and come upstairs. I remember when Efrem Zimbalist was dating her and would call—I was absolutely in love with that man. I had the most gigantic crush on him and *77 Sunset Strip* became my very favorite television series. I thought he was just perfect for Mother because they were both very conservative.

I'm not surprised that she never remarried because she loves her home in Santa Monica—behind the gates with her privacy and animals—and messing around in her terry bathrobe. As a kid I remember her greatest joy was to come home from the studio, take off her makeup, get into her old scroungy bathrobe—the comfortable one—turn on the television, make popcorn, and be very unglamorous—her reward to herself for working so hard during the day.

Mom never wanted to be a movie star—she wanted to sing grand opera at the Met. Her beauty and gorgeous figure deflected her from that career and brought her to films instead. It is ironic: With her chest measurements, tiny waist, and sexy appearance, Mother was never a sex goddess, although she probably had measurements that outdid most of the sex queens of her day.

She never wanted me to have the wrong idea about image. She was stern with me, but inconsistent. I can see that because of the things I do differently with my own children. She, for the great part, did not follow through—letting me get away with things sometimes and coming down hard for the same infraction at other times. I never do that with my own children.

She dramatically instilled God and morals in me, although there wasn't any set religion as such. She taught me to be kind and loving and to do good things and good things would come back to me. We were never churchgoers. I had an aunt who was Jewish, an uncle who was Roman Catholic—and I was exposed to it all. Mom always told me that someday I could make up my own mind what

Patricia Johnston Towers ☆ 61

I wanted to be once I knew what the alternatives were, though she was a Christian primarily.

She believed in good old-fashioned spankings when they were called for. My mother is a very physical person in every sense of the word. I had a big mouth, which she found intolerable, and I'm lucky I still have a lot of teeth. Any kind of sass infuriated her.

There were times when she wasn't fair—simply because it wasn't expedient to be so. A lot of parents have that problem in Hollywood. They have pressures and whole careers may depend on what seems like a small decision. All too often the child hears, "Don't bother me right now, I have problems of my own." Children have problems, too. That remains in my memory as being "unfair." But such things happen in a household when one parent has all the responsibility of bringing up the children. It isn't fair.

I will say "I'm sorry" at the drop of a hat. Mother was never one of those "I'm sorry" people. She would let me know in various ways, but just could never bring herself to use those exact words. As a Libra, I'm sure that I'm more aware of that kind of injustice and possibly overly sensitive in that area.

All my life, my very closest friend has been Mario Lanza's daughter, Colleen. Her mother and my mother were pregnant together, so it was just inevitable that we be like sisters, since Mom and her parents were so close. Kimi Moore, who is now married to Gregory Peck's son Stephen, is my second oldest friend from childhood. I'm so proud of her—she has just sold her first movie script, *Little Darlings,* to Universal as a starring vehicle for Tatum O'Neal and Kristy McNichol—just did it all on her own and never told a soul until it was done. And there was Francesca Hilton who has done quite a bang-up job of surviving the shadow of being Zsa Zsa Gabor's daughter. I love Francesca, although when we were kids she was three years older than I and I recently read she is now four years younger. But that's my friend Francesca!

As a student I seemed always at a point of physical and mental exhaustion from all that was going on in my life away from school. If my family had problems, they became my problems—when I should have been concentrating on studies. Like mother, like daughter. And Mother depended upon me more and more as I grew older. I stopped being the child and suddenly I was another semi-adult standing there, quite capable—when she would allow me to be—of helping with a lot of the problems. But Mother has always been a very independent lady and never liked to share her chores, which I found very frustrating at times. On the one hand she would want me to be the young adult, but then on the other she expected the little girl. The adult—who was mannered, charming, and used her head—and the sweet little girl who never opened her mouth and never had an opinion of her own. It got to a point where I was unwilling to be Kathryn Grayson number two. There was the conflict—the age-old problem between mothers and daughters. I never wanted Mother to father me. I think she misunderstood her role there and took that as a sign of weakness—that if she ever admitted she wasn't both something would happen that would be drastic. That was a total misconception of her role in my life. My mother is from the Old South and was never brought up to be weak simply because there was no man around; she was brought up to be in charge. Right or wrong, be strong. I do believe she has unknowingly made me a better mother because of that heritage.

I think "normal" people understand what it is to support a child when you're on your own and unmarried, but I don't know if they see it from the point of view of a star who is constantly under a magnifying glass, trying to keep her head straight and trying to hold her ego in check while all the adulators are fawning all over the place. It used to turn my stomach.

I saw the phonies around Mother and I tried to become her eyes and ears behind her back—to see what the smiling faces were up to when they weren't bowing and curtsying before her. I heard them tear her apart backstage—people she worked with. For some reason people seem to think of kids as a fifth wall in a room and because of that I used to get an earful of the backbiting that went on between some of the people who called themselves "friends" of my mother's.

She didn't always want to believe the truth. When she had problems we would sit down and talk it over—she would ask my opinions. By the time I was in high school and not a very silent young lady, I spoke my piece and we would have some rather knock-down drag-out verbal battles because she didn't want to believe what people said behind her back.

There were times when Mother deserved criticism. She could be difficult if she was troubled. The temperament I saw was the kind associated with not being on time and letting people wait for her—the star syndrome that so many actresses seem to adopt. It was like saying, "I am the star and if you care for me you'll wait for me," and I told her I didn't like it, many times.

Mother could be a hellion. One time she marched into the inner sanctum that was Louis B. Mayer's office at MGM and flatly announced she was not going to do a song she had been assigned to sing in a film. Storming, she said, "Mr. Mayer, I won't do this." She tossed the music down on his desk. "This is a piece of junk. I will not do it. You can have it. Throw me out of the studio if you wish, I don't care. But I am not going to sing this trash." What she didn't know was that the man who had written the song was sitting unobtrusively to one side taking it all in. She was totally embarrassed when she realized later on that she might have hurt the man's feelings, but when she was letting L.B. have it with both barrels, she didn't think of that. She never changed her mind about the song.

Mother did not believe in forcing me to mingle with the children of other stars simply because everybody else was doing it—like the birthday parties where the kids didn't know one another from Adam. Consequently, I never developed the popular, "I don't mix with the plebeians" attitude. I am, however, ferociously loyal to my friends, many of whom I have known from childhood.

Since I had appeared in public from time to time—joining her onstage as I grew up—it was inevitable that I would eventually have more important roles. After I graduated University High School in 1967, the tempo picked up. The following year we toured the Far East together—Japan (where they had a piano on rollers at Tachikawa Air Force Base), in Quonset huts, service clubs, and plenty of rain. I was gathering confidence in my own ability. Mother and I had done *Camelot* together at Melodyland and I'd performed Wendy in *Peter Pan* at the Carousel—both theaters-in-the-round near Los Angeles. At that juncture, my heart was already set on a career of my own.

Career is one thing. Dating—that is a whole other world. Oh, my Lord! I had my first unchaperoned date in broad daylight at the ripe old age of sixteen and a half. It was for a matinee—the first time I was permitted to meet a boy alone. Can you imagine that kind of maternal strictness? I told you Mother was old-fashioned! It was never that I wasn't trusted; she didn't want others to think she was "loose" with me.

I didn't have to be told that if I got into any kind of "trouble," it would reflect on my parents' names. I already knew that—I'd read about star kids in trouble and the headlines were so big with the celebrity parent's name, it became difficult to find the name of the child.

There were four proposals proffered before I became engaged to Bob Towers—who is a very talented actor from the Broadway stage. When I first told my mother that I was engaged she had a rather, "Oh, that's nice" response—but almost immediately added: "You better start making plans for the wedding." Once she realized I was serious, however, she began throwing up the roadblocks.

Her reality was, "I am losing my baby." It was difficult for her, I'm sure, because all those years all we had was each other—and she could see that dissolving into nothing. She didn't, I'm sure, want me to do what she had done with her first marriage. She and Johnny Shelton had eloped—and later divorced. Her parents were quite puritanical and locked her in the bathroom so she wouldn't get out of the house. She merely slipped out the bathroom window—and eloped with "Uncle Johnny." I, on the other hand, had no such intentions. Whereas I was a little bit square, Mom had been quite a rebel as a young girl. So whatever misgivings or distrust she might have had were not of me as much as her memories of herself at my age.

No matter. Reality prevailed and the wedding preparations were made. Suddenly her temper flared from out of nowhere. She had difficulty handling *that*. People think of her as sweet-voiced little Kathryn Grayson—the soprano. What they don't know is that she has a temper, when riled, like the Los Angeles Rams' front line. When that didn't work she tried a more subtle approach. "I'll build you a guesthouse in the back and you can live there," she cooed.

"But, Mother," I reasoned, "we don't want a guesthouse in the back. We want our own place." We weren't kids. I was almost twenty-one and Bob was thirty-three. And so it went. It took a long time for her to accept my being married. After ten years and two grandchildren, however, I think she's grown fonder of Bob than she is of me—just crazy about him.

Dad, on the other hand, had no objections whatsoever. He journeyed from Puerto Rico (where he was living at the time) for the wedding.

I grew up in Hollywood and in a celebrity world, but I think I was just as much a product of a post–Civil War antebellum period as of twentieth-century Hollywood. Louis B. Mayer once told my mother, "Katie, if you'd only been born sooner you'd have been a great Scarlett." Mother agreed with Mayer. She is the typical southern little flower with a backbone of cast iron: "Never let anybody step on you, and don't be a withering idiot."

In 1970 I was approached by a producer who was putting together a show featuring the children of stars for Las Vegas, to be called *The Name's the Same*. The premise disturbed me. I'd had a lot of hurt as a child and was very lonely—because many of the other kids did not understand being a star's kid. So when this show came up I let my guard down because I didn't think anybody would consider exploiting stars' children the way this was done. It was politics at its worst. Your talent didn't count. I was not aware that being buddy-buddy with the producer and who you slept with would decide how much you were given to do in the show over talent—until this came up. It was a big disappointment. I was billed as Kathryn Grayson's daughter, which hurt me because of my dad who, to me, is the star and I don't like him forgotten either. My father was not a flash in the pan "no talent." My name never was Grayson—it was Johnston. I don't want to offend my mother, but I'm proud of both my parents. So much for name exploitation.

I wanted success for everybody in the production who worked hard and earned it. Francesca Hilton was laughed at by some of the others when she first came to rehearsal. "Gabor's daughter—what the hell can *she* do?" someone quipped and others laughed. May I tell you that she worked harder than anybody else, knowing she was in that position, and came off very good because she tried her best to make the show a success.

That experience in Las Vegas caused me to put away my show business ambitions for the moment and concentrate first on starting a family. I have no intention of giving up my career permanently. Once my children are older, we'll see.

Because of my stringent upbringing, I never was involved in premarital sex, never took drugs, and I respected my parents. Also, with my mother's background I think it is to her credit that she raised me without prejudice.

Looking back, I'm amused by her futile attempts to explain the facts of life to me. She laid everything out in very sweet, gentle terms—but not very graphic and I totally misunderstood her parables. Such phrases as "the father plants the seed," left me in a quandary. I was thinking in terms of a shovel and a hole in the earth. She was being totally honest with me but not going far enough with her explanations. I had a lot of male cousins, but I knew nothing of how their parts worked. It was only later I figured out the whole truth about the male/female relationship.

I was afraid of Mother until I reached the age where I realized I was just as strong as she in my character and makeup. Mom never backs down from anything, but she respects strength.

Obviously aware of her own human frailties, my mother hoped that I would somehow avoid them. She attempted to steer me away from falling into lazy patterns. I'm sure she made concessions in her personal life. If she did, she never made me feel guilty about it, never gave me the old cop-out, "If it hadn't been for you . . ." which I've heard from other Hollywood parents all my life.

Sure, I missed doing some things other kids my age did, but only in a physical sense—only in that I wasn't there. I'll never regret being exposed to classical music over rock 'n' roll or being taught morality and manners rather than being permitted to "do my own thing" and taking up with the free sex and drug scenes. No, thank you. I had wonderful parents, and my mother especially worked hard trying to be what she thought a good mother should be. I think she succeeded beyond her fondest dreams and I will thank her for the rest of my life.

Marlene Dietrich in a publicity still from the late twenties or early thirties.

Courtesy of Larry Edmunds

Michael Riva in a pensive mood at the beach. Note the strong resemblance to his famous grandmother. Marlene Dietrich.

Michael Riva's grandmother—the incomparable Marlene Dietrich

Courtesy of Larry Edmunds

5

☆

Michael Riva

Nobody needs to be told who Marlene Dietrich is. She's an international work of art. Her grandson, Michael Riva, is the son of her only daughter, Maria, and her husband, William Riva, an art director at NBC Television in New York. Michael is third-generation show business.

Needless to say there is a lot of Marlene Dietrich in his personality (perhaps because she had a lot to do with his upbringing) that well matches the remarkable resemblance he bears to her.

He is quite boyish in manner yet gives one the impression that he takes his work as an art director (like his father) quite seriously. He was recently the art director on Robert Redford's films *Brubaker* and *Ordinary People.* I don't think he takes himself that seriously. There is that bit of mischievous boy in the man that attracts others. We were instant friends.

I had a wonderful childhood and I miss it a lot. Nothing about it was normal. With Marlene Dietrich as a grandmother, how in the hell could I ever have had any kind of "normal" childhood?

My father was an Italian immigrant who started out as a sketch artist and became one of the best art directors in the country. He met my mother, an actress, at Fordham University where he was employed in the theater department. She was there, for some unremembered reason, sitting in the audience, while he raced about the stage giving directions to everyone. She has told me she thought he was quite handsome, very angry, and very mean. Nevertheless she turned to someone sitting next to her and said, "That's the man I want!" My father reciprocated by falling in love with her and they were married, whereupon they set up housekeeping in an almost cold-water flat about fifteen feet from the Third Avenue El in New York City.

Because of our proximity to the El I grew up loving trains. I would often wake up in the middle of the night and rush to the window to watch the trains zoom by. I loved the sound of the wheels building up to a clacking crescendo as they passed in front of my window and then faded away into the Manhattan symphony of sounds and smells as the train rumbled on to the next station.

After we became more affluent and moved uptown to East Ninety-fifth Street, I still had my trains. Our house was only a block from Park Avenue where the trains emerged out of the bowels of the earth and I used to go there with Mother to wait for the trains to come hurtling out of the tunnel and off to God only knows where.

Mother was often away when I was small, working as an actress in theatrical productions and in summer stock. My father pinned a large map of the United States on the wall of my room, which I shared with my younger brother Peter, and placed colored pins at the places my mother was at any given time. I got to know when the pins started back the other way that Mother was on her way home again. She became a pin on the map. I never questioned my father's diligence as he positioned each pin because I didn't think he particularly liked the idea that she was gone.

When Mother was out on the circuit, my grandmother took care of me most of the time, because my father worked. When my parents took a late honeymoon they left me with "Maus" (which I've always called my grandmother). Maus remembers it as fondly as I do. We understood and loved each other from the very beginning. She delighted in walking me down Park Avenue in my pram as people stopped to ogle the glamorous Marlene Dietrich showing off her grandson. She was never ashamed of her grandchildren. That was part of her glamour and she always wore it well.

Always a firm believer in fresh air, she would keep me out in the sunshine for hours. She said it was good for me and there's never been *anything* too good for her grandchildren—especially me, because I was the first. She has always doted on me. That became an embarrassment as my brothers began to feel some resentment toward me.

When Maus would come back to New York after being out of town I'd run to greet her at the front door. She always came in with big fur coats and was always very warm and cuddly. She would hug me for the longest time. We still hug like that. What warm memories! A normal hug with her was two or three minutes. Being small I could jump up and wrap my arms and legs about her. I loved that. My mother didn't love it. My father was not too sure. Mother, I've decided, was probably jealous. She's had problems with Maus from time to time. They have not always been close. Mother is the middle generation—which may be the biggest generation gap of all. My wife and I have discussed that. We're both the oldest and both have had the same problems—being put down or berated by our parents, primarily because of jealousy. We were getting all that love and affection from grandparents of which they felt cheated. That has always been a problem between my mother and me.

Not so long ago, Maus and I had a little tiff and didn't communicate for a couple of months. My mother enjoyed it thoroughly. Speaking to her on the phone about it I said, "I think I'm going to call Maus and tell her I love her—that everything's OK."

Mother said, "No, no. Why would you want to do that? You'll just end up with the same problems." I did call her, however, and everything is just grand between us now.

After my brothers were born, Mother gave up the road to bring up her family. Yet she was determined not to lose touch with the theater and the people in it. Consequently, Christmas became a tremendous social event at our house. Stars dropped in like snowflakes against the windowsills. I loved stars—and I still do. The entire living room would be closed off for a week before Christmas week in preparation for the big event. I remember polishing the Christmas balls individually every year and *House Beautiful* sending photographers over to take pictures.

There was always a tremendous party on Christmas Eve and we boys always dressed in our best clothes. Whoever was in New York and was connected with the theater was there. Noel Coward was a regular at our house and always attended those parties if he was in the city. There were always more men at the parties than women—

especially if my grandmother was there. Although my mother was a star in her own right and the star of her parties, my grandmother was a show unto herself. When Marlene Dietrich walks into a room it doesn't matter who else is there. Maus understood her devastating effect on people and would discreetly retire to the kitchen, where she was more comfortable anyway. She loved to prepare food and send it up on trays for the guests.

When I lived with her in Paris as a teen-ager, we would go visiting her friends and she would invariably make her way to the kitchen and take over. We'd go to parties with people like Orson Welles or Jean Pierre Casal as guests and my grandmother would always go off to the kitchen.

I loved meeting all those famous people. What a fantastic way to get an education! Maus, on the other hand, is not a very social person. She is definitely not a sitter. She likes to be active. She is, on the other hand, generous to a fault. Loves to give. I have been fortunate in being the number-one recipient of her generosity.

My youth was very New York-oriented. My god-father, a publisher—and, I believe, a onetime lover of my grandmother's—was a wonderful man who always treated me with warmth and kindness. He never quite related to me, however, because children just were not his thing. He was an exquisite-looking man. A White Russian with white hair, he was very tall and wore the most beautiful clothes I've ever seen on any man. He had a magnificent home and a butler who waited on him. A confirmed bachelor, he was always in the company of gorgeous ladies. One of my great pleasures as a young boy was riding around with him in his limousine. He was very much like the uncle who loves to hug and kiss the babies and then hand them back.

Michael Riva ☆ 75

I have another grandmother. My grandmother Riva has always simply been "Mama." She is traditionally Italian and a terrific grandmother. It was always wonderful to see this stoic, pious individual doing the same things every day. I can still see her sewing dresses for anyone in the neighborhood who brought them to her. Although she and Maus were totally different personalities, they got along fabulously. Maus had a sister in Germany, very much like Mama—both Old World people who were never afflicted with any social diseases like stardom. Maus, because of that, always liked Mama and treated her like a sister. Despite what you might think, they never crossed culinary swords. When Maus is in the kitchen, her attitude has always been, "I am the star in the kitchen, so get the hell out!"

Growing up, I was sheltered by my parents. We were a big family. There were four boys—Peter, Paul, David, and me. We were close-knit and Mother wanted us to have the most structured education. It was not unusual for her to take us on outings to the Museum of Natural History or anyplace else she thought our education might be improved.

There was, for me, a negative side to this closeness. We boys were included in everything our parents did—including their fights and arguments. Ordinary family fights, just as I have with my wife, Julia. Fights that never seem to resolve anything.

My father never took kindly to the fact that he was wrong sometimes. I never ever heard him say, "You're absolutely right. I was wrong. I apologize." Not in my entire life. Therefore, I learned as a child how to tiptoe around my father. Mother, who was the champion tiptoer, knew how to manipulate my father for us—and get us what we wanted. She would have made a great agent.

I've always loved my father. In the past ten years he's

become somebody who I also like a lot. Always an eccentric individual, he worked like crazy—often going to the studio at six in the morning and not returning until midnight. He was a very dedicated man—dedicated to what he had committed himself. Yet he didn't like the work itself and finally gave up his position as top art director for NBC Television Network.

I never planned to follow in my father's footsteps. It was his example that fascinated me. He took half of one of the family living rooms as his study and it became the crazy place in the house where he was always erecting models of future television sets. I eventually succumbed to that fascination. He never pushed me. Mother wanted me to be a writer—something for which I've always had a flair. I may utilize that talent somewhere in the future.

Being the oldest, I was often lonely. Expected to be a good example to my brothers, I had a lot of pressure to do and be a lot of things that I didn't want to do or be. I saw my friends at school doing things that I couldn't do. Being denied some of these normal outlets, I developed certain aberrations, indulging myself in fantasies that were totally my own. I loved playing war and dressing up in combat uniforms. I would sometimes get up at four o'clock in the morning and roam the streets of New York pretending I was shooting the enemy. I had a lot of hostility that needed an outlet. Riding my bike around New York City at that early hour was an education in itself. I saw the most amazing things: policemen passed out in their own vomit from drinking; gamblers and hoods making deals—and hookers. Incredible stuff. My father eventually discovered my secret and rode out with me several times. That was fun.

I made friends with some of the angry young men who came from poor neighborhoods into our area to play stickball and intimidate the wealthy. I enjoyed being with them, and one, an Italian named Dennis, took a liking to me and gave me a leather jacket as a gift. I reminded him of his little brother, who was in prison. Though it scared me to death I felt I was in touch with reality being with them.

I can still see my mother's shocked expression when I walked into the house wearing my studded street-gang jacket. "You can't wear that . . . that . . . ." She never quite got it all out, but I got the message and never wore it again. All I ever wanted to do was be a regular kid, but that seemed an impossibility.

My father was strict with me. Again, being the oldest I had to deal with him ahead of my brothers. I was the great experiment in child raising. Every once in a while, when my father's anger got out of control, he would hit me. Once, he tried to spank me with a hairbrush. He hit me across the fanny with it twice and started to cry and hug me. It didn't hurt that much and the whole thing seemed ridiculous. Yet it was a moment when we were very close and I remember it with great fondness.

When he got around to Peter I had already been the route and knew what was coming. It was easy for me to tell him to go to hell in my mind and go on out and enjoy myself. My ability to handle that aspect of my father may have been one reason I didn't get along very well with Peter. That, coupled with the feeling that Maus didn't like Peter very much, most likely had a lot to do with the chasm between us two brothers.

Maus's influence was very strong in our family. Stronger than anybody else in my family will readily admit. Peter never had my gift of charm. I would say to my grandmother, "Oh, you look beautiful. You look wonderful." Peter said, "You know, you look older than you actually are." One doesn't say that to anybody, let alone a star of Marlene Dietrich's magnitude. Naturally it hurt her feelings. She might say, "Out of the mouth of babes comes the truth," but she loved my truth better than Peter's.

Mother sensed her dislike of Peter and always came rushing to his defense. Mother had been overweight as a child and Peter was also heavy. She identified with his problem and cuddled his fat. Peter and I were pitted against each other from a very young age because of the family politics being played by adults. For instance, he was very good in mathematics. Math was my worst subject. I was straight A in English. Peter was terrible. Somehow my mother managed to make me feel that English was not so important, but that math was quite essential to survival. Consequently, Peter was a better student in her eyes and got most of her support—and none from my grandmother who was becoming more and more, in my mind, my mother.

I loved school. It was an opportunity for me to be with kids my own age and there was a real sense of glory in not having to come home for eight hours or being obliged to report in to my mother. One of the greatest things that ever happened to me was the privilege of living in New York as a kid and not in Shaker Heights or Beverly Hills. I don't think I would have tasted any reality in those places. In New York you can't avoid it. When you walk along the street and step in dog shit—that is New York and an inescapable reality.

I was beaten up on the streets with great regularity. Older boys would lay in wait for the little rich kids and take our money, jewelry, clothing—anything. Once I made friends with Dennis, who gave me the jacket, life became easier for me. He gave me my first taste of chewing tobacco. He tolerated me and I felt important.

I always attended private schools. In my seventh-grade year the family took a cruise on an Italian luxury liner to Europe where we spent the summer. My parents were also looking into Swiss boarding schools for Peter and me.

The trip was a wonderfully enlightening experience. It was the finest time I ever had with my parents. In Venice there was a special moment with my father. He woke me up at six one morning and said, "Come on, let's go." It was the beginning of a habit we developed over there of getting out and walking together early in the morning.

Our home on the Upper East Side of Manhattan was a very large brownstone on Ninety-fifth Street. We lived next door to a "spooky" house where it was rumored that all the occupants had committed suicide. The most recent had been a famous artist who slit his throat. Across the street lived June Havoc, an actress and former burlesque queen, who was Gypsy Rose Lee's sister. Vince Sardi, who owned the famous New York theatrical restaurant, was also a neighbor. He loved kids and we all loved him. I remember the time he brought a double-decker bus over from London to advertise his restaurant and took all of the kids on the block on the first ride. It was fantastic—except that the Upper East Side wasn't quite ready for double-decker buses and we carried a few long hanging tree limbs along with us.

Maus lived in a glamorous penthouse on East Eighty-first Street. I often walked there from school. The doorman, who knew me, made me feel important. Oh God, how I loved that apartment up there on top of the world with mirrors everywhere—her bedroom was mirrored from ceiling to floor and she had gleaming hardwood floors. The apartment was extremely French with dark Chinese pieces for effect. She opened the doors to the fire escape off her bedroom and allowed me the supreme thrill—the view.

After returning from Europe that summer I realized I was a lot older than I had been at the beginning of the trip. I was fourteen and I'd toured Europe and seen a lot of different ways of life. I genuinely felt more grown up. My father must have sensed that feeling because I remember we walked into the house and he asked me to get him a beer from the cooler. When I brought it back he said, "Do you want to take a slug?"

I said, "Sure," and took one. That was my first drink except for small sips of champagne at Christmas or New Year's Eve. It was a very special time for me. His gesture confirmed my feeling. I *was* older. That was just another step toward my maturity.

I also remember another incident. When I was twelve I woke up in the middle of the night after my first wet dream. Waking up and feeling a warm milky mixture covering my stomach and wondering what the hell had happened—then smiling and knowing I was no longer a child.

Mother was very good about sex education. She told me everything I wanted to know. She also taught me about being gentle with girls and loving with gentleness. My father never talked to me about sex. I'm not sure he knew how. Thanks to Mother I always felt at ease about sex.

Later on, when I spent a lot of time with Maus, Mother would become very upset. Being a glamorous lady in the theater, Maus was always surrounded by numerous men who just happened to be homosexuals. Mother suggested that the association might change my sex orientation—and said so on more than one occasion. She would become quite angry when I spent more time with Maus than she thought was prudent and would ask, "Are you going to become one of her little homosexual friends?" Ridiculous. By then I was old enough to know a few things and homosexuality never frightened me. There have been many men whom I've known and loved and always hugged. In Europe, you hugged people and kissed men and I never worried about it. I love talking about this because I'm quite proud of it. I love being able to talk about my feelings. I wish to God that more of my men friends felt the same way.

My early months in Swiss boarding school were rough ones. Everyone spoke French. I knew only English. I was thrust into a situation with a lot of strange and similarly disgruntled students and subjected to the most God awful harassments, beatings, clubs, and cliques. Eventually I adapted, but not before I had learned to endure a lot of pain—both of the heart and body. Weekends I spent with my parents who had taken a house in a nearby French village to be close to me and my brother Peter who was in another Swiss school. Weekends I spent with my family. On Sunday night they would drive me back across the border to my dormitory.

The school was almost Prussian in its austerity. If you delayed getting your hair cut to the proper (short) length, you were hauled before the headmaster after dinner where, before the assembled students (who were allowed to tease and laugh), the headmaster seemed to take great glee in shaving your head. Talking in study hall would get one a good ear-boxing. Upperclassmen delighted in the privilege of beating up the younger boys. It was often ugly, bloody, and messy.

Boys' schools are supposed to be great hotbeds of homosexuality. During my six or seven years there, I can remember only one incident where two boys were caught together by a teacher who apparently enjoyed relating their deed to all the other students. It was like throwing Christians to the lions. One kid was so badly beaten by other boys he had to be hospitalized. The other, for his own safety, was expelled. The second young man, once released from the hospital, was strangely allowed to stay on. I am sure the cruelty involved affected me because he became a friend of mine two years later. The incident had a great impact on the school; the following year nobody wanted to talk about it. Most of them felt dirty for having participated in such brutality.

That kind of pressure was constant. Any homosexual feelings I might have had—which were totally natural in an all-boys school, and I had lots of them—could not be realized because of the restrictions. I was definitely more concerned with self-preservation. Consequently, I slept with every girl I could find—maids, German girls across the tracks—whoever was available.

School life improved. I moved up another echelon on the seniority ladder and gained additional privileges. I became one of the four guys who set the trends during my last years there. I began to spend vacations away from home. The year I was to graduate several of us spent a month in Majorca at Easter vacation time where we got drunk every night, danced, and made out with the girls. I was seventeen and it was wonderful.

What I thought was my last year turned out to be something else. I thought I was going to go out on a crest of popularity. Instead, I was involved in a disgraceful incident that was disastrous for me and a total embarrassment to my family. It was right after my hot trip to Majorca. One night, about a dozen of us blackened one another's faces with lampblack and set off to raid the dormitory of a nearby girls' school. Our headmaster and theirs had been at odds with each other for years and raids were common. Nobody had ever been punished for making the raids in the past.

That particular night, everything went wrong. We intended to paint a naked statue of a man blue but something went haywire, and it turned into breaking windows and general vandalism. As we walked across to the other school, another group of boys approached the dorm from the opposite direction. Soon there were twenty or thirty guys and what started off as an innocent foray became a debacle. One boy went up the hallway inside the dorm and girls started screaming and yelling bloody murder. That brought the headmaster, who unloaded a shotgun of buckshot into the rear end of one young gentleman as he ducked over the balcony.

Smeared with blue paint we all laughed, once we were back in the safe confines of our own dorm. I didn't expect a big stink. While the other boys burned their ruined clothing, I just tossed mine into the closet and forgot about them. When the police came the following day with the headmaster from the school next door they searched our quarters and I was the only one caught "blue handed." My gesture of supreme martyrdom was to not reveal the name of my coconspirators. I started out wanting to be liked by everybody and ended up screwing myself.

My parents were called in and there was a helluva meeting in the headmaster's office, which ended in my being expelled.

I was driven away from the school in disgrace. A disgrace that was short-lived, I might add. The headmaster had made a deal with my parents and I was allowed to repeat the year and graduate with the next class. The humility of having to redo that whole year with a class lower than my own was very demoralizing. But it taught me a lot. I learned more from that year than from all the other years of my schooling there.

On the flight home, I took my seat across the aisle

from my father and settled in for what I expected to be the silent treatment. He ordered champagne and then started to smile. He just couldn't keep up the pretense any longer. The truth was, he was proud of me. So we all enjoyed champagne together and it was OK. Mother hugged me and let me know I wasn't a total outcast. Maus thought it all totally normal—a good red-blooded American boy going over to raid a girls' school was nothing to get excited about.

That extra year was the beginning of my future. I had been humbled, but I was the "old" guy on campus. The young kids thought I was a god, so I lived like one. I had my own room at the end of the senior corridor where we always had rap sessions going. Boys came to me with their problems. It was a wonderfully fulfilling experience.

I started a drama club and produced Sidney Kingsley's *The Detective Story,* a vehicle in which my mother had starred on the stage some years before. Drama really turned me on. I don't think I'd ever seen more than one or two of Maus's films, but one of my classmates was Joseph von Sternberg whose grandfather was the director who brought my grandmother to America. Together we saw all of her films and I discovered a new dimension to my enthusiasm for her.

By now, my parents were living in London and I went to live with Maus in Paris where I enrolled in college following graduation at Le Rose. I commuted to London on vacations and holidays. I spent time with friends, many of them from my Swiss school days. Since hashish was so plentiful in London, it became the thing to do. It was a new era in learning about other people. Wonderful guys and girls. It was 1968: Free love and all that jazz was popular. We smoked hash every night. My father would smell the aroma filtering up from our basement where I held forth and it made him quite nervous. I never could talk to him about it. I love him, but he just doesn't understand

In 1970, I moved to California, entered a common-law marriage (we're now legally wed), and spent a couple of years at UCLA. I studied writing and lighting but eventually dropped out because the place was overly populated and I had my own ideas about how I wanted a scene shot.

Another aspect of my life that came too late and didn't last long enough had to do with Maus's husband—my grandfather. He owned a chicken ranch near Los Angeles, which was his life until the earthquake of 1971 tore everything apart. I have recollections of him being at our Christmas parties in New York when I was young, but I believe he felt out of place there. After my first visit to his ranch at the age of twelve, I was in love with his world of animals and gardens, his chickens and goats and his little house. I knew him as a nice old man who loved me, loved to talk, and loved to tell me stories.

Maus always came out to see him. He was her ace in the hole and they loved each other very much. I think he was the only constant thing she ever had. He was a lonely man in many respects. He met the young Marlene Dietrich in Berlin, took her home, made love to her one night, and they got married. Following my mother's birth, she went to America with her friend and mentor, director Josef von Sternberg in search of a film career. I believe she was either working on or had just finished *The Blue Angel* at the time. Von Sternberg loved her and would have done anything she asked. He and my grandmother got along very well—both Old World people who understood each other. My grandfather followed Maus to America, bringing along their small daughter—my mother.

I don't think anybody knew my grandmother was married anymore. People just assumed she was divorced after their early years, but they were married until his death not so long ago. He did a number of things in the film industry in America, but he was sort of an outcast. Fame and fortune hit my grandmother like a ton of bricks and she enjoyed it from the beginning. It was never his kind of life. He would later return to California with another woman with whom he had fallen in love, and my grandmother, never a sexually jealous woman, bought a ranch with him in the San Fernando Valley where he settled down to raise chickens. He was never happier than at the ranch. Eventually he and the lady parted, but he lived on alone at the ranch.

On his early visits to New York I don't think he ever felt quite good enough about himself to say to me, "I'm your grandfather." So when I came out to visit him, it gave him the opportunity to make me proud. We got up at six o'clock—just he and I—and went to feed the chickens. Like I said, he was Old World and I definitely was not. He could, however, be very childish. The same morning that we fed the chickens and collected eggs, he discovered a sick hen. To show me bravado and machismo, he removed the sick layer, put her in a funnel, and cut her head off right in front of me like it was a normal everyday thing to do. For him maybe it was, but he knew full well that it was probably not the best thing to do in front of an impressionable twelve-year-old. I was horrified. It created a suspicion in my mind that wasn't allayed until I came back to California to live and found the other side of him.

He was a connoisseur of everything—life, ladies' breasts (he loved ladies' breasts), good wines, flowers, candles. I identify with that. I am now better able to understand why he and Maus never divorced. In their unique way they loved each other and were good for one another.

So much for my past. My future is ahead in the motion-picture industry as an art director. I'm now our third generation in the business. I don't know how Maus feels

Michael Riva ☆ 87

about that, but we talk films constantly when we're together. We critique, we have the same tastes in theater and movies. When I lived with her in Paris, we saw incredible pictures and cried together through many of them. I'm very fortunate to be who I am and to have had the parents I had.

I'm blessed in a special and loving way to be Marlene Dietrich's grandson. To the world she is Dietrich—to me she is simply Maus and has influenced my life probably more than anyone else.

Young Julia Warren with grandfather Harry Warren
Courtesy of Julia Warren Riva

Julia Warren (about three years old) and doll house
Courtesy of Julia Warren Riva

6

☆

Julia Warren

Julia Warren, the granddaughter of famous Tin-Pan Alley and film songwriter Harry Warren (currently enjoying renewed fame with the smash Broadway hit *42nd Street*), is married to Michael Riva, grandson of the legendary and gorgeous Marlene Dietrich. They were married, in fact, while this was being written, after eight years of cohabitation. That is indicative of Julia's personality—doing things on the spur of the moment.

She is unlike any other of Hollywood's Children in this book, in that her sense of humor supersedes all else in the glitter world in which she grew up. In her quick wit and ability to dissect her Hollywood surroundings with the precision of a surgeon, I was reminded of the early Jean Arthur.

Knowing all the weak spots in the Hollywood balloon, she doesn't hesitate to poke her finger through them. Her celebrity upbringing belongs to the genre of Shirley Temple coloring books. She confesses that hers was the life of a princess but considers herself "a spoiled rotten celebrity brat."

There is no way Julia Warren can be considered a contemporary "anything." She comes from a background of the zaniest, wackiest Hollywood era and for her, time has stood still in freeze-frame.

Note: Harry Warren died after this chapter was written.

Harry Warren was my grandfather. As the eldest of his grandchildren I was indulged to nausea. Daddy (which has always been my name for him) was part of the movie songwriting team of Warren and Gordon (Mack Gordon). They produced some of the great song standards of the big musical pictures of the forties—the Glenn Miller pictures, Judy Garland's *The Harvey Girls,* Alice Faye and Betty Grable pictures—I mean big stuff. By today's standards he would be right up there with Manilow, McCartney, and Lennon.

Since my early years were spent with my grandparents, I was exposed from the beginning to all of the then- (and many even now) great names of Hollywood. It was normal at our house to have Cary Grant or Nat King Cole for dinner, along with dozens of other household names.

We lived in a big house in Coldwater Canyon where all our neighbors were famous people. Harold Hecht, the producer who made all those marvelous films starring Burt Lancaster, lived across the street.

I shudder when I say this, but I had the life of a spoiled princess, attending all the parties Daddy gave and allowing everyone to make a big fuss over me. We had big parties with big stars lounging and littering and impressing one another. I have never been able to remember who anyone is, and even then was often mistaken for a snob because of my bad memory. It is a family joke that the only star I ever was able to recognize was Cary Grant and him only because he worked with Daddy for so many years. Daddy claims to be eighty-six, although I think he lies about his age.

Daddy is a very old-fashioned Italian man and I've been told many times by others that he is a genius. On the other hand, my husband's grandmother is Marlene Dietrich and that's like having an institution for a grandmother. I love her too. She's a wonderfully incredible lady who is a star at all times.

My grandfather used to have a bad temper. Just terrible, always screaming and yelling. I still fight with him about that, but I'm the only one in the family that dares to. It is a concession he allows because I am his favorite. I even chose to have his last name instead of my father's. We had celebrities on both sides of my family. My grandmother on my father's side was Janet Beecher—a renowned actress in her day. Sorry to say, my father didn't inherit any of her genius—theatrical or otherwise.

Show business fascinated me as a child, but not for the usual reasons. I wanted to be a writer, but writers must work hard. I preferred being the princess. My early life was all in the Hollywood tradition. The right schools. Buckley, Hawthorne, and Marymount. The Beverly Hills litany of education. I attended school with the children of celebrities and some became close friends. Billy Gordean whose father was an agent, Steve Lovejoy (Frank's son), Pat Tone whose parents were Franchot Tone and Jean Wallace (now Cornel Wilde's wife). We were all close. In high school my very best friend was Tisha Sterling whose mother was Ann Sothern. Her father, Robert Sterling, is now married to Anne Jeffreys. Hollywood is largely a place of "I used to be married to's."

Celebrity life affected me greatly. It totally unprepared me for real life. Even today I cling to those drawing room standards of living. I mean, when you sit down to dinner you have beautiful linen, with beautiful service on the table; ladies are always elegant and one has servants (which I don't have now). I'm forever making jokes about the servants: "My God! Where *is* Hudson when I need him?" You know, the butler and the upstairs/downstairs maids. Those are things one was taught to take for granted. Not having them right now is nothing. Just a bagatelle until I can get it together and live decently.

Since I'd been brought up by Daddy and Grandmother, I assumed I'd always live with them. When I left my grandparents and went to live with my mother and stepfather I resented them not providing me with all the comforts my grandparents had given me as a child. I thought I was entitled to all that. I didn't know people *worked* to get money, because show business is a place where you never realize people actually work. I mean, Daddy went off to the studio and when he came home everybody stayed out of his way so he wouldn't blow up. In the evening everyone had a cocktail and things returned to the status quo. Life was one big sophisticated game. At cocktail time my grandmother would make a little fake old-fashioned for me. She'd go to the bar, put in the grenadine, mash up a sugar cube, and slice in an orange. I don't think she intended for me to hurry up and learn to become an alcoholic. It was just a social amenity of the times, and then you lit the fire in the fireplace and everybody discussed the events of the day. It was all very Noel Coward.

I am still amazed that I am able to go to the market or do mundane things because my life was going to the English bakery for bread, the tea shoppe, and schlepping to Saks to try on the latest imported designs—or in those days one shopped for fashions at Don Loper's. I loved to play saleslady and try on hats while my grandmother browsed through designer clothes. Left to myself I'm sure I'd have worn maribou robes—I mean if the feathers didn't get up my nose—and float around in "at-home" outfits. I was Shirley Temple in all those poor-little-rich-girl movies. My dollhouse was big enough to walk into. We had four dogs. A Great Dane, a Scottie, a dachshund, and a "something else." I had a nurse and there was a chauffeur. Also, there was Lucille Laurens, our housekeeper and cook to whom I would write severance checks and pretend to fire when she did things I didn't like. She just laughed at me. My office was the guest bathroom next to my grandmother's den where she had a large desk at which she conducted her personal business.

My grandmother would give me her old checkbooks and I'd pretend to be running the household. My desk was the toilet lid and I had a little stool. I was Little Miss Marker and all adults were Kay Francis. In the morning my grandmother would be served her tray and Ed, our butler, who was Lucille's husband, would bring my tray with my own chocolate pot and my own cup.

Moving in with my mother and stepfather after all that spoiled indulgence was like moving in with the poor relations, even though Mother did have a big house in the center of Beverly Hills. I was traumatized. I couldn't believe I was going to live with these peons who didn't have breakfast in bed. And Mother committed what to me was a mortal sin. She proceeded to have more children. There wasn't enough for me, much less any more. I think I've spent my entire life trying to get back to that little girl in Coldwater Canyon with all the servants and "things."

I found every excuse not to live with my mother. Adjusting to reality was painful. Daily I would phone my grandmother and ask to be brought "back home." She would pick me up "for the day" and I'd stay as long as I could. It took me away from what I considered the boring and ordinary existence of everyday Beverly Hills living. I fancied myself as a kind of Beverly Hills Scarlett O'Hara, vowing never to go hungry again.

You have to love Hollywood to live here. One either accepts this town and the people in it, or gets out. I grew up here and I'm used to everybody being the way they are. It is normal for me to see somebody walk into a party with a riding crop, doing the Darryl Zanuck thing or being very funny. It is a hammy industry and people are always "on."

There is a sad side to my Hollywood story. Many cannot handle the celebrity merry-go-round and it kills them. Some of them drink their lives away. Others do themselves in with drugs. I've been lucky to retain a sense of humor about Hollywood and that, probably more than anything else, has saved me. You simply cannot take it seriously. It is a fantasyland.

The real world to me, nevertheless, is this town. I don't know what other people do. Life is a Hollywood sound stage and has always been for me. Where else could one live that the worldwide headline gossip is about your next-door neighbors? It is an international soap opera. The Beverly Hills housewife with all her Gucci clothes. The rich are different. F. Scott Fitzgerald said that and he was right. For instance, my grandmother said to me yesterday, "It is all relative. Someone says twenty thousand dollars to you and you fall on the floor. Someone says it to me and I say, 'So?'" Money means nothing to her, and I've discovered not having it is a disaster.

I'm saddened that so many of the kids with whom I grew up, friends whom I love, get so spaced-out on drugs. There's the daughter of a famous show business couple, now divorced, who is a very special person to me. She's so out of it on drugs that I just want to pick her up and bring her home with me and say, "Shhh. Don't cry. Don't let those people hurt you." Hollywood is a small town and the next thing you know my husband was working on a film with her father's current wife. There was a cast party and the father came. I wanted to hate him for neglecting his daughter. At the party I started thinking about all my school friends who aren't here anymore: Jack Wrather, Peter Boyer, Gregory Peck's son, Jim Arness's daughter. People who killed themselves one way or another. The poor little lost children of Hollywood. At thirty-five I can compile a long list of my contemporaries who couldn't handle the pressure of celebrity life and are gone. It is frightening.

We are a forgotten generation, the children of stars. There's a picture in Christina Crawford's book of her birthday party and I looked at that picture and thought, My God! I've got pictures just like that. I've got the Crosby boys at my party with the same kind of center-piece. I know exactly which toy shop it came from—Bernie's Toy Menagerie on Rodeo Drive where they had a lemonade tree and a lollipop tree that made the rounds from one star's home to the next. Not too long ago I went to a party at that very house [in which the Crawford children grew up]—a big bash. Some star groupie had bought the place and threw a party and there I was. Déjà vu. They were serving drinks from the Crawford Theatre and then to read a book like Christina's and to have all those memories come rushing back. Memories of birthday parties where you rode around on ponyland horses and the mommies and nannies who oo'd and ah'd and everything. Maybe they cared and maybe they didn't. You never really knew.

We all wore the same kind of clothing, same name brands, living our lives to grow up and get paged on the loudspeaker at the Polo Lounge. Not being allowed to be "normal." I read about Brian Wilson of the Beach Boys who ran away from home and was playing the piano and singing for cigarettes and booze in a Manhattan Beach bar. I couldn't even do that. Still can't play piano because I wouldn't study and nobody disciplined me to make me do it. Oh, they screamed and yelled, but it didn't mean anything to me and that was the end of it. I resented my stepfather. To me he was obnoxious, always practicing his musical instruments and going to the studio to record.

How can anybody ever think I had a normal life? Right now I'm trying to recall thirty-four years of Disneyland. I remember a lemonade stand made at the studio, which the butler would set up for me, and I'd sell lemonade in front of Daddy's big house in Coldwater Canyon to his celebrity friends and neighbors. I remember my sister and brother being into the Davey Crockett thing, along with Harold Hecht's little boy, Duffy, who was the same age as my sister Jophie. They all went to Western Costume and came home with little coonskin caps and fringed outfits of the frontier. How much did it cost? Whoever thought about cost? You just thought about telling the butler you'd sold all your lemonade and to please go back into the house and make another pitcher.

How many times did I hear my mother say, "Oh my God, but those kids have *so many* toys . . ." and then we'd be off to Bullock's Wilshire at Christmastime to clean out the toy department. When Mother was married to Johnny Hacker, the musician, I hated Christmas. Johnny always brought home some cheap tree that was so short we had to put it on a box to make it look the right size. But at Daddy's house—wow! Every Christmas, the gardener put up the big lights on the pine tree in the front yard and inside we always had a giant tree with a beautiful centerpiece, which was like a church with red windows. When wound up it played "Silent Night" and was all bright and glittery.

Christmas at Daddy's was a genuine social event with lots of presents. We didn't have presents at my mother's house. That was OK because I was kind of a snob anyway. I was always comparing her house with Daddy's. I must have been a real pain in the rear to her.

I never got into drinking, although it was all around me. I associated liquor with sociability and never realized it could be dangerous (although my father, of whom I knew very little, died of alcoholism). I couldn't imagine people doing things to harm themselves—like being on drugs all the time or drunk.

I was a little princess and lived a sheltered life. My grandmother was always full of fears—always warning me to watch out for white slavers and kidnappers, but nobody ever said beware the alcoholic. I grew up in a town where the police knew you and if you were out doing things you ought not to be doing, they brought you home.

I grew up in a plantationlike atmosphere where ladies were ladies and gentlemen were gentlemen. It was a cavalier world. Young girls tittered and laughed on the staircases in crinoline skirts. They went to the proper places and grew up and married the proper men. Their obituaries told about all the organizations to which they belonged.

The sanity in my life came from Lucille Laurens, our housekeeper. Lucille was a proper black lady from Louisiana. Most of my favorite memories involve her. My favorite occupation was polishing the silver with Lucille. She was the most incredible lady I ever knew. She came from New York with my grandmother and went to gourmet cooking school after their arrival in California. She ran our house with an iron hand. You didn't mess with Lucille—not ever!

From Lucille I learned all those delicious traditional

southern dishes—pigs' feet, black-eyed peas, corn bread, and greens. She had her own mint patch for mint juleps. Lucille was just as much a snob as any of us. Maybe more so. You didn't dare do anything unladylike around her. That would get you a whack up the side of the head with her wooden spoon, an ominous weapon that appeared from out of nowhere when needed. But bless her, she taught me how everything was done. Although I never did menial chores, I was taught by Lucille that you bloody well better know how to scrub floors before you tell anyone else how to do it. She was a star in her own right and knew it. She used to scream at my grandmother that she was turning me into a spoiled brat.

But I loved Lucille. As she worked she would tell me stories about her grandmother who had been a slave, while I tagged along awestruck at such seriousness. She taught me that ladies never got drunk and fell over; that ladies were always charming and good hostesses. I was amazed when I grew up and found there were people who didn't like black people. Daddy had dozens of black friends.

To me my grandmother was "Majo" and *The Hollywood Reporter* was "The Gog." I delighted in going out to the mailbox every morning to get Daddy's Gog. I read the headlines and considered myself well informed. I couldn't imagine anybody who didn't read *The Reporter* every day because everybody I knew treated it like the Bible.

Back to Lucille. I must tell more about her because she was the single most important influence on me as a young girl. She was real. She was normal. She taught me always to take something if I went visiting and always to thank God that I was who I was because but for the grace of God I could have been "some pickaninny in a corn row." How would I know if I turned into a pickaninny? Lucille assured me it was the pits.

To Lucille, a cardinal sin was anything in a package. All food had to be prepared from scratch. I learned how to make the stiffest egg whites and the best mint juleps in Southern California. She was pure hell on trashy people. God forbid I should take up with riffraff. She looked down her nose at some of my grandfather's guests whom she considered trash. People she said didn't know anything except what money could buy. Thanks to that gracious lady I know how to work a mangle, that Mrs. Wright's Blueing is proper, and to this day I still use White King "D" because that's what Lucille used.

I grew up in an atmosphere where men screamed a lot, and Daddy was a dedicated screamer. One of my earliest memories is of him coming to steal me away from the nurse when I cried. He would take me to bed with him in his bedroom, which always smelled like cigar smoke. There were fabulous snow-white sheets and a down comforter—and books. Dozens of books and an incredible reading light by the side of his bed.

Because of my exposure to this kind of life, to me money is something you get and use to get *things*. I have no fear of getting old and not having money. One simply does something to get it—have garage sales or make do, or whatever. My grandmother was very poor when she was young, yet she is a classy woman. I always remember her wearing magnificent clothes.

I might have been a star in my own right by now if I'd been allowed to be. I lived next door to Norman Foster who produced the famous Mr. Moto pictures. He wanted to put me in one of his films and my mother wouldn't let him. I've never forgiven her for that.

My whole family was wonderfully wacky. I remember when someone sent my grandfather one of the first commercial television sets, and always fancying himself a mechanically minded individual, he ruined it with his "know-how." Another time he applied that same genius to repairing the toilet and flooded the house.

I had some rocky times as an adult because of my upbringing—like fighting for my own identity. My grandparents sometimes have not shown much respect for me because I haven't always conducted my life the way they thought I should. Our arguments have usually ended with each side calling the other crazy. Somehow we have survived.

There were other traumas. I remember how sad we all were when Richard English died. He was a writer who lived down the street and had been blackballed during the McCarthy era. I was never able to get the whole story about all those un-American activities hearings because the newspapers were hidden from us kids and we weren't allowed to watch anything about it on television. Too many people close to our family were involved. I have often asked my mother what she was doing during those days and she always manages to be a little vague. It must have been a trying time because it seems to me that everybody was accused of being a Communist.

Parties at our house were a riot. Daddy always invited all those old chorus girls, and after a few drinks somebody would start playing the piano and somebody else would sing a song from an old show—or a new one. Life in the creative hills of Beverly. It was the formula used in so many of the old Donald O'Connor pictures.

And then there was Judy Garland. She never missed Daddy's parties because he wrote so many songs for her. And, oh God, whenever Judy came to your house you locked the medicine cabinet because she went through everything looking for pills. She made great gossip for all the women and I listened as intently as a spoiled princess is supposed to.

Life was fabulous. Today when Daddy takes us to Trader Vic's he tells great stories about the "good old days" when the place was a chili joint. He still refers to bars as saloons and thinks twenty-five dollars is a large amount to give you. Meanwhile, my grandmother whispers to me, "Don't worry. I'm going to buy you something nice with all the money I sneaked from Daddy."

My grandmother has a mind like a steel trap. She invested her money in the stock market and bought land—not as much as my mother, but she probably could have bought Beverly Drive if she'd wanted to. For a lady who came from no place, she's done pretty damn well. She saw the opportunities and used them. Mother took them for granted and simply got lucky. Thank God those two women knew how to do those things, because Daddy couldn't care less about money. My grandmother always said it was a good thing he could write songs because she was convinced he was totally worthless and inept at everything else.

The most horrifying experience of my life, being sheltered as I was, was marrying for the first time without any real knowledge of what I was doing. I'd had teen-age romances, of course. When I was in eighth grade I was madly in love with Pat Tone and also madly in love with Steve Lovejoy. "Our gang" all learned about sex during that period of time—myself included. Danny Thomas's daughter Teri, my best friend for a long time, taught me to smoke. They lived around the corner. But my God, it wasn't like today: You were instructed to be a virgin your whole life practically—so it wasn't easy to get around or to be wild. We had to sneak.

I was the sheltered one, but I think truthfully my mother wanted to be the baby and still does. She wants to be loved, to be somebody's doll—but who doesn't? I find it interesting to see my mother still having that incredible need for approval from her parents. Having parents in this business is difficult. I understand that. They don't do anything like "normal" people. Movie people are only normal when they're with other movie people. Before my husband joined the union he was the art director on a lot of low-budget pictures and was always taking the furniture out of our house, throwing it on his truck, and taking it away at odd hours to use on the sets of his film. It was not unusual for me to be out in the driveway at four in the morning screaming, "You son of a bitch, bring that back. Don't take my couch. What the hell do you think you're doing?" I thought we'd never fit into the neighborhood. But I hung in there because I wanted my son, Jean Paul, to grow up in a halfway normal neighborhood.

I must be a Hollywood traditional. I'm on my third husband. My first marriage was to a man who was French, worked in films with Roger Vadim in Paris, and didn't want babies. We had a son. We divorced. The second time around I married a celebrity baby. My mother gave us a beautiful wedding, but it wasn't until after the "I do's" that our problems emerged.

Then I met up with Michael Riva and we started playing house—and told everyone we'd been secretly married. His mother wasn't too hot for us being together, either. It didn't matter. We were in love. Still the flack flew from his family. They were sure he had taken up with a wanton woman. They were wrong about that, but we managed to keep our common-law marriage perking along for eight years. Now it can be told because we're going to get married—finally—and take that skeleton out of the family closet.

Michael and I share a fantastic experience, both being the eldest grandchild of a famous person. Although

I doubt anybody's fame could equal that of Marlene, who is an absolute riot at all times. You should see her at the beach. There's nothing funnier, because you can't see her at all. She appears with big dark sunglasses and all bundled up—like a butterfly in a big cocoon. Most of her family lives in fear of her. Michael never has—and she loves him for it.

She didn't know much about me when she came to Los Angeles one Christmas for a visit to her husband's chicken farm in Sylmar. The whole Riva clan was there and Marlene made a very pointed negative comment about me. I shocked all of Michael's relatives when I looked the famous Dietrich eyeball to eyeball and said, "Don't ever talk to me like that. I don't care who you are or what you've done. You're just Michael's grandmother to me." We've been the best of friends ever since. When Michael first told his family (falsely) that we were married, she wrote him a one-liner about me and asked, "Can the girl cook?"

There is a lot about Marlene that people don't know. She's got stories that are hysterically funny and she is an extremely practical woman. When she comes to Hollywood, she stays at the Beverly Wilshire Hotel and we go to her. Stars like Dietrich don't go out to people's houses. She'd probably drive me crazy if she came in here and started nosing around.

Michael came from a matriarchal family. He hasn't changed a bit. He would leave every decision up to me if I allowed him to. He's the biggest coward in the world. Of course, I was properly trained for all this, so I am not surprised. If I told him there was a murderer at the door he would say, "I'll hold your coat. I'm sure you can handle it."

In spite of all that celebrity snafu in our backgrounds,

we've had a good eight years and I think a happy marriage ahead. Sometimes it's like the War of 1812 between us, but then I grew up with that, too.

If I have an idol in all of this celluloid and tinsel they call Hollywood, it is Madame Goddam—Bette Davis. She's the epitome of everything I'd ever want to be. You'd have to drive a stake through her heart at midnight to kill her. She's such a bitch and I love it.

I'm not saying I'm pure, because I'm not. I'm a celebrity brat and I love this town and one day I'm going to write my own book about it. I'd like to tell about all the sob stories I've heard—listening to world-renowned celebrities crying "I cannot afford this," and the next day you run into them at Holly's Harp buying every expensive dress on the rack.

It's all bullshit, but such wonderful bullshit.

Marty helps his father celebrate his birthday.

7

Marty Haggard

Born while his father was serving time in San Quentin Prison, Marty Haggard's earliest memories of his parents are of them fighting. Although he tries to project a calm exterior, the pain of those early years filtered through during our conversations. Merle Haggard is a country-and-western superstar. His son, Marty, is a cautiously quiet, soft-spoken young man who bears a remarkable resemblance to his famous father.

At the time of our interview Marty had just been released from the Kern County Jail in Bakersfield, California, his crime little more than protecting his mother, who has also had her share of trouble.

To me, it seems unusual that Marty Haggard has survived at all. But he has. He recently stepped away from a singing career that, according to his manager, Jim Wagner, would have grossed him close to a quarter million dollars in 1981. He now works as a hydro-blaster in the

Bakersfield oil fields at a rough job most men don't want. He and his girl friend (soon to be married, they say) have a new baby girl. That, he says, is the reason for taking a breather from the entertainment world where he seems destined for success. "I want my child to know who her father is and do the things a father and daughter do together. I never had parents in that sense and I don't want my child to be cheated like I was."

Marty thinks positive about the future and I wish him well. He is a bright, warm, sensitive, and caring young man.

My parents were Merle and Billie Leona Haggard. Today my father is a superstar. My mother isn't faring so well. Even so, things are better now than they were when I was growing up. I had a terrible childhood. My earliest memories are of my mother and dad fighting. If there was even the slightest problem between them it ended up in a fight. I was very small and always frightened when they fought—afraid somebody was going to be hurt badly. To this day I cannot stand to see family fights.

Outside of that, I don't remember my father at all until I was almost twelve years old. Just can't remember his face or him being around. I was six or seven years old when they broke up and still there is that blank. It was not the first time my parents broke up—just the last. They'd been through it all before. He was just starting out on the road toward what would eventually be stardom as one of the all-time greats in country-and-western music. His first single record, "Sing a Sad Song," made the charts and brought in enough money to finance a road trip for him.

My mother was a pretty straight lady until she met my father. Dad was in and out of jails most of his young life. As a matter of fact, from the ages of fifteen to twenty-one he spent more time behind bars than he did on the street. He went about everything the hard way and everybody concerned paid a heavy price, including his wife and children.

My grandparents were Okies who moved to Bakersfield, California, during the Great Depression of the thirties. Dad's father died when he was nine years old and he was brought up without a father. Grandma tried. A widow with three kids in hard times. Dad had a hit record about that very thing, called "Mama Tried." He was always her favorite and still is. No matter what kind of trouble he got into, in her eyes it was always somebody else's fault. "Merle was a good boy," she used to tell us. "He just got in with a bad crowd." She had difficulty accepting the fact that my father had his own mind and was usually the leader of whatever trouble was coming down.

There are four of us. I'm twenty-three, my sister Dana is twenty-four, Kelly is nineteen, and Noel seventeen. When my parents divorced, the courts awarded custody of their children to my father's mother. Dad was fresh out of prison and Mom was going through a period where she was in and out of trouble, caused mostly I think from the breakup of her marriage and my father's lack of responsibility about supporting his family. You can't very well take care of your children while you're in San Quentin. The judge felt that neither of our parents were fit to have us at the time, so we went to Grandma's.

I didn't like what was happening to me and was miserable. I'd been jerked away from both my parents—Dad was on the road and Mom in trouble. I soon forgot what my father looked like. I felt only bitterness, hurt, and anger.

Grandma's house was nothing like ours. For one thing, there was no nonsense and no fighting. The sudden change in lifestyles had other effects. Grandma was strict and very religious. Mom and Dad were the exact opposite. There was no transition period. Grandma had her rules and we were expected to abide by them from the very first day. I fought her system for a long time and I'm sure there were times when she wondered if I wasn't taking the same troublesome path my father had gone down ahead of me.

I used to think I hated her. Now I appreciate the effort she made on my behalf. She was my roots. All I saw at the time were rules and regulations, complicated by my own form of rebellion. I was quick-tempered, like my father, and she was a master at tossing cold water on that.

Grandma was old-fashioned in her religion so we went to church. Not just on Sundays, but sometimes three or four times a week. I learned a lot about hell, fire, and brimstone and the loss of my eternal soul if I didn't straighten up my ways. I feel certain, however, it was her attitude that kept me out of any major trouble during those difficult years until I went to live with my father again. In school I managed to stay out of the middle of bad situations, but I often instigated them—then would stand back and watch. Nevertheless, I did get into fights. Maybe that was a result of watching Mom and Dad fight, but I would rather believe it was a way of taking out my frustrations away from home and not bringing them back to my grandmother's house. I didn't make friends easily. I'd loved my parents and lost them, so maybe I was afraid of losing friends. I honestly don't know.

I went to school in Bakersfield, lived with Grandma, and saw very little of my parents. Sometimes I'd see them at Christmas. Sometimes not. Dad was working. Always away doing personal appearances or in the recording studios cutting new albums. They tell me he stopped in once in a while during brief trips to Bakersfield, but I don't recall any of that. Maybe I don't want to. Too much hurt. I think I listened to his music, but somehow I never associated him with being a performer. Didn't associate the music with him. I didn't know anything about his fame and fortune. I was in junior high school when he recorded "Okie from Muskogee" and that was the first indication I had that he was somebody important in the entertainment world.

Everybody knew about that song. It was one of the biggest things to happen in music that year and it created all kinds of controversy for me. Kids at school were talking about it. They knew who he was. They knew more about my father than I did. Grandma never told us anything. She didn't want us to be a part of whatever he was doing. She tried to keep us away from his spotlight and succeeded in doing just that.

I hadn't seen my mother for a long time. No one would talk about her in front of me. None of it mattered to me. Grandma was my anchor. My parents were just names that people talked about.

When my father remarried I knew nothing about it. I heard about it when someone asked, "Hey, did you know your father got married?" I soon found out that he had married singer Bonnie Owens who had recently been divorced from another country-and-western hero, Buck Owens.

I was living in Oildale at the time with Grandma and my brother and sisters on Yosemite Street. My father, I discovered, was living only four or five blocks away with his new wife and I remember one day just hopping on my bike and going over to their house and seeing her for the first time. I didn't know who she was. It meant nothing to me, but suddenly there she was—my new stepmother.

I walked into their house and my father was lying on

Marty Haggard ☆ 113

the couch from which position he introduced me to Bonnie. I didn't say anything. The whole idea was weird and it is difficult for me to explain now my feelings at that particular moment. It takes weird folks to become celebrities in the first place. I think they are like that before they get into entertainment—just folks who don't do anything like anybody else.

Dad had never done much in the way of supporting his children—didn't at all for a long time after we went to live with Grandma because he didn't have the money to launch a career and support a family at the same time.

Just before "Okie from Muskogee" was recorded I went to live with my father, still not knowing exactly who and what he was. Most kids like to be at least a little bit like their dads. I didn't even know how to play a guitar. Didn't own one. Wasn't interested. I didn't have what might be called any kind of "normal" relationship with him until about six years ago.

I was in shock when it finally got through to me just who and how big my father was. Not being brought up in that atmosphere and having it all come down on me at one time without any warning was like being struck by lightning.

There was some flak from my schoolmates. Most of them were into pot and even though the song was an anti-marijuana message they liked it. They also liked him. Mostly they teased me about it. A handful of guys wanted to start trouble, but I handled that without getting too ruffled or frustrated. My father was making his great social statement about mom, apple pie, and the flag, but I had my own social problems to contend with.

Thanks to his big success with that record I stopped being just Marty Haggard and was known to everyone as "Merle's son!" That's the biggest pain for me even now. I hate to be introduced to anybody as Merle's son Marty. I'm proud of what he's done, but gee, don't people have sense enough to realize I'm me?

I didn't have many friends. Maybe one or two. I never brought anybody home from school. I didn't want to have to explain who "we" were and why our family life was so different from that of "normal" families. Mostly I just had acquaintances and since I wasn't sure why they were friendly toward me, I became very cautious.

Even living with Dad and Bonnie, family was neglected in favor of career. I've met a lot of entertainers over the years, and believe me, career comes first, last, and always. My dad was no different from the rest of them. Grandma, however, always had faith in him—even when he didn't have faith in himself. But Dad was her baby. Always was and always will be. If I ever said anything bad about him she would get madder'n hell at me. Still does. In her presence you don't talk about him, no matter if he's right or wrong. I know she's been disappointed in him at times about some of the things he's done, but she can live with that. He was spoiled by her and mistreated in ways, too. She loved him so much I think she was jealous of other girls. He was never allowed to have girl friends over because she resented them. I think she contributed a lot to him being so damned rambunctious and headstrong. She spoiled him and then again she didn't.

I'm told she gave my mother a bad time from the day my father took up with her. Even tried to whip her with switches. I can believe that because she used to use switches on us kids. Made us go out and cut our own switches and they had best be good ones or she'd go out and cut one even bigger. She comes from Cherokee stock and I guess the Cherokees must have invented switches. A lot of Cherokee grandmothers use them.

Anyway, I was thirteen years old and living with Grandma. Mom was still in some kind of trouble and I just decided I wanted to go try it with Dad. My sisters and brother came with me—and so did Grandma. We all moved in with my father. It was hard to realize that I even had a mother because I had Grandma. I knew I had a dad, but he was really a stranger. I liked my mother, though. The few times I did see her while I was growing up I could tell that she was likable. She seemed to act a little crazy, but I learned later on it was just the way her sense of humor came out. I had difficulty convincing myself that, yes, this was really my mother. I'm still trying to get used to having parents.

In the past three or four years I've been around my mother more than any other time in my life and with all her hang-ups and problems she really does have a good heart and loves me within her capacity to do that.

When I moved in with Dad, Bonnie was working with him on the road, singing backup harmony. "Okie from Muskogee" became an overnight explosion. I had only recently moved from Grandma's humble, religious atmosphere into the crazy world my father lived in and all of a sudden we were all uprooted again.

From the time my father was a young boy he fished up in the Kern River above Bakersfield. High in the mountains east of Bakersfield the river flows almost creek-like into Lake Isabella, which was created by damming up the river. Below the dam for thirty or forty miles the river flows on into Bakersfield and some of the best fishing in California is to be had there. It was Dad's lifelong dream to be able to build a house up in the mountains next to the river so he could fish whenever he wanted. He'd just never seemed to get enough money together to do it. That all changed.

Within two or three months he had drawn up his own plans for the kind of house he wanted, bought the property, and, in less than a year, built a mansion in the canyon by the river—with his own private lake. It was everything he had ever wanted for his private self. We moved into the new palace, lock, stock, and barrel. I changed schools, which wasn't bad because I was entering high school. One advantage in going to a new school in a new district, especially with the fallout from "Okie," was that I didn't have to see or deal with the kids who had given me a hard time in junior high school because of my father.

There was another twist in our lives. We now had servants and special people to look after us. A butler and maid—husband and wife—were brought in. Very sophisticated people who were all "yessir" and "nosir." Those people didn't know anybody like us existed, I'm sure. To them, we must have looked like a bunch of ignorant hillbillies who struck oil in our backyard. We all had a rude awakening as to what the "other" side of life was like. They had worked for Harrah's Club at Lake Tahoe and Reno. Whenever stars came to appear at one of the clubs this couple served as maid and butler during their stay. They came into our house trying to be very straight and because of that we were all unhappy. It was uncomfortable because we simply did not live like that—only they didn't know it. We were just plain people stuck in the spotlight.

For the first time in my life I started meeting big names in the entertainment world. That was something else that seemed to go with all my father's newfound success and money—always the power of money. People are attracted to it. It became common to have houseguests like Glen Campbell (and he was hotter than hell at that time),

Marty Haggard ☆ 117

Johnny Cash, Dolly Parton, and others. During the summertime Dad started taking me out on the road with him from time to time and I guess I've probably seen everybody in the music business once or twice—and a lot of movie stars. It affected me like it would anybody else—I was a fan. I made a big fuss over them in a private way. I wouldn't let them know it, but I was really excited. I couldn't understand at the time why people got excited about Dad, however. I didn't see him as such a big star. He was just my father.

I met many people in the sports world, too. They impressed me most of all—especially baseball stars. I'd played baseball when I was younger and Dad sponsored my team. It was called Hag's Boys. But don't think he threw money away on his children. He didn't. He sponsored the team, but he wasn't often a spendthrift with us. He claims he didn't want us to be celebrity brats—spoiled celebrity brats. I think he succeeded. He could have gone hog wild like other country-and-western stars I know. After "Okie from Muskogee," money was flowing like fresh water from a well. He has bought me a couple of cars, but outside that he hasn't been excessively generous considering his status and his financial position. I don't mind that at all, though I must admit it used to bother me some in school when I'd see kids whose parents had far less income than Dad getting new cars every year. Wreck a car—get a new one. That was the plan. But not for my father's children. He didn't believe in that and I think I agree with his thinking. One day he'll probably be gone and I'll have to fend for myself, so I don't want to become his dependent.

There have been times when I really needed something but couldn't ask him. I'm sure he would have helped me out if I'd told him, but one of the most difficult things for me to do is to ask my dad for anything. I'd rather do without. Maybe it is because I have a deep-seated belief that I don't need him. That I can do it for myself. (If that's so, I hope I am outrageously successful.)

I've said that the big record and the big money that followed changed our lives. It had a profound effect on my father. In a very short period of time he went from being just a singer to a big-time singing star. We went from average home to million-dollar mansion—from the average life to the lap of luxury. There was no break-in along the way. Dad suddenly went from plain old Merle to Mr. Merle Haggard. He was so hung up on himself that it was miserable being around with all the hangers-on fawning all over him and telling him how great he was. He's coming out of all that now—but I think he has to fight what the "yes, Merle" people around him are constantly whispering in his ear. I've been exposed to a number of superstars and they all have that albatross around their necks—the parasites whose very existence depends on staying in favor. They're nauseating.

I like to think I had something to do with bringing him back to earth some of the times he was up there in the clouds playing Mr. Celebrity. He'd get a little bit fed up and start acting like a father. "Hey, Marty," he'd say, "wanta go fishin'?" Those were the fun times—I think the only real father/son times—for me. But then, he'd turn the whole thing around. Completely wipe out the token relationship and I wouldn't see him again for six or seven months, living in the same house together throughout. He's always been inconsistent, especially as a father. I try to accept that in him now because he just can't seem to help being who he is.

Because of our circumstances, we kids have always been close. When we didn't have a father or mother we had each other and we were always supportive of one another. (I'm especially close to my older sister Dana.) Dad never should have fathered any of us. He doesn't have time for family. Never has had. It is all career. I've tried to fight any resentments I might have of him—and there have been some. He has a bad temper and so do I, though I work constantly to control it. About once a year he used to really let me have it; we would be arguing and I'd push the point beyond his endurance. It wasn't your average belt to the butt—it was an old-fashioned ass-kickin'. He used to whip me pretty much all over the house while I just tried to keep from getting my teeth knocked out. We had our last fight about three years ago just before I started out on my own music career. Outside of the whippings he gave me as a kid, it was the first time we actually made physical contact—a genuine fistfight. He tried to hit me, I blocked his punch, and we ended up on the floor where I got a wrestling hold on him so he couldn't hit me. I didn't want to hit him, but I was determined he wasn't ever going to lay another hand on me. I think it worked because he treats me more like a man now. He talks to me in a different tone. I respect him because I can see that he now has respect for me.

I was never comfortable living in the same house with my dad. I had no life of my own. Everybody in the house was an extension of Merle Haggard. That was it.

He never could leave work at work. He brought it home with him. Music was his mistress. His children were summoned up to his room when he got home to hear his new session or a new song. I was maybe thirteen years old and hadn't been living with Bonnie and him long. I didn't give a damn about his music. None of us cared about it. We weren't interested. I remember when he was learning to play the fiddle, being forced to sit and listen to him and listen to those old Bob Wills songs. At that age, how in the world was I going to be interested in songs from the forties? Now I am, then it was pure drudgery.

It was after a road trip with my father in my late teens that I was forced to start thinking about my own future. Rather, it was the end of the trip for me. We were in Odessa, Texas. I got into a fight with my little brother. Dad objected, I talked back, and the next day I found myself no longer a member of the group. He was pleased that I stood up to him—hurt, too, maybe. He now says he did it for my own good—so I'd go out and do something for myself. Maybe so, but I managed that on my own. If he wants credit, that's OK, too. I was flat broke and his band leader slipped me some money to come home on. That's when I picked up my first guitar, learned to play, and formed my own group. I had to show him he wasn't the only member of the Haggard family with talent.

In the meantime, while trying to find out who I was, at age thirteen I was visiting a friend's house and was introduced to the world of sex—seduced by the eighteen-year-old baby-sitter. I hope she enjoyed it because I didn't know what was going on. I was a frightened young boy in the hands of a girl who knew all the moves and had all the answers. I never saw her again and would probably have been embarrassed if I had. Up until then, I had had no idea such things existed. Nobody ever told me about it really. I'm still shy with girls. My stepmother, Bonnie Owens, tried to explain something to me once, but it just didn't register. She was spouting off about how a girl gets pregnant and I just blushed and said, "Yeah, yeah, I know," and got the hell out of there.

When I went out with my own group I was able to profit from the advice my father gave me about being on the road. By that time, he wanted to make me happy—

wanted me to do what pleased me. And there was an advantage in being his son. He was (when he wanted to) able to introduce me to some of the right people in the music business. But he couldn't sing for me, he couldn't play the guitar for me, and he couldn't make people buy my records. His name got me noticed. The name alone, out of curiosity, will get people to come out and see me. They'll come and look, but if I can't perform it won't help.

My father could have influenced MCA Records to record me, but he didn't. He had nothing to do with my label. Jim Wagner of American Management (my representative) did that for me. I was signed with Dimensions Records and almost didn't get the contract because Merle Haggard was my father. What changed their mind was an article somebody at the record company read—an interview I had done with somebody. And even then they only decided to *listen* to me. I was told right out they didn't want a "junior" with a big bad attitude. Most ambitious children of celebrities seem to have that in their personal makeup and it turns off entertainment executives. I had no problems with that and it didn't damage my ego.

I learned the hard way to protect my feelings. I thought both my stepmothers cared about me. Bonnie, as far as we knew, was the closest thing we'd had to a real mom in a long time. She and Dad were married for ten years. She had two children of her own, but by the time we moved in they were older and gone. Bonnie Owens was good to me while she was married to my father. After their divorce I didn't plan for anything to be any different—nothing was going to change between us. But it did. Bonnie stopped treating us like her children. She became distant. Stopped calling. I guess she stopped caring. It was a shock. The one most affected was my younger brother because he was quite young when they were married and she was the only real mother he ever knew. She just seemed to wipe the slate clean. It had happened to me once before with my own mother, so I handled it better than my brother who, because of that rejection, has a calloused attitude toward women and is having a hard time handling that.

My father has somewhat of a reputation (much of it simply untrue and exaggerated gossip) as a wife-beater. I'll defend him on that most of the time. I never saw either him or Bonnie raise a hand to each other. They never even shouted at each other in front of us kids. That shows me that if he had beaten the other women in his life (including my own mother and current stepmother) they must have done something to provoke him. Ten years of peaceful living with Bonnie was no accident.

In spite of being the child of a celebrity, I grew up without drugs. I don't like grass. I can't drink. It has only been in the past year that I've developed any kind of enjoyment from any drug—cocaine—but I can't afford that either financially or emotionally. I have a new baby and that has changed my life and my thinking.

It was an accident—a mistake—Shree and I having Dani Rene, our little girl, but it was the best mistake I ever made in my life. My background certainly wasn't a great advertisement for home and marriage. I was born while my father was in prison and was two years old when he came home. I was told about that and it haunted me throughout my young years before I went to live with Grandma. All I ever saw were unhappy people, fighting all the time. People who didn't really want kids.

I would like to continue my career, but not if it interferes with my relationship with Dani Rene and Shree. I don't want to become a celebrity in the sense that there isn't anything I can't do or get simply because of my name. I've seen too much of that "American Royal" way of living. I just want to perform my craft, do a credible job, and get paid for it. I'll always just be plain Marty Haggard—because I know superstars today who were nobody ten years ago and now they're demanding that everyone call them Mister.

I want to be loved and respected, not idolized.

Jack Haley. Sr.. reads from *The Wizard of Oz* to his then eight-or nine-year-old son. Jack Haley. Jr.

8

☆

☆

☆

Jack Haley, Jr.

Son of a most beloved father, Jack Haley, Jr., has inherited his father's moxie for the world of entertainment and is happy being the man behind the camera.

As a producer and director he enjoys almost as much prestige as his famous dad who was immortalized as the Tin Man, one of Judy Garland's friends in *The Wizard of Oz.* His productions of *That's Entertainment* (Parts I and II) have garnered him public, industry, and critical acclaim.

Unlike many of Hollywood's children, Jack Haley, Jr., is secure about himself, his work, and his place in the world. As a youngster growing up in the streets and hills of Beverly, something of a cross between Tom Sawyer and Little Lord Fauntleroy, he appears to have retained only the positive aspects of the celebrity carnival. Candid about himself as well as his family, I seriously doubt there is a Haley "closet" and if I am wrong about that, I am convinced the only "skeletons" are plastic ones left over from some long-forgotten Halloween escapade.

Jack Haley, Jr., is the contemporary film-maker, not a neurotic misfit trying to escape the shadow of a father beside whom he stands quite tall and proud.

I think I began to realize that my environment was a little peculiar when I was four or five years old. I would see my father on a motion-picture set performing with Shirley Temple and she certainly wasn't treated like the rest of the kids on the block. Other boys' parents weren't doing that. Even at that early age, one begins to have a perspective that things aren't the way they are with everybody else.

One of my first horror experiences involved seeing my father on the screen in a film called *Wake Up and Live,* which he made with the late Walter Winchell. Dad played an usher in a radio station who also happens to be an excellent "swoon" or "croon" type singer. He becomes a phantom singer (the essence of the plot). At an audition he begins to sing and the special-effects department creates his point of view of the microphone, which suddenly puts on a devilish face and begins to breathe smoke. In the film my father is obviously terrified, so I, watching my father become terrified on the screen, became terrified too. I was carried out of the theater kicking and screaming. The first of many emotional traumas I would suffer as a youngster growing up in the film capital!

My father prepared me for the *Wizard of Oz.* I was just starting to go to school when the picture was made. He took me on the set a couple of times, which was fun because both Bert Lahr, an old family friend, and Ray Bolger, who was like an uncle to me, were there. I saw the various stages of makeup and enjoyed it all so much I began to take my friends with me to watch my father,

Judy Garland, and all those wonderful people play make-believe. When Dad was busy rehearsing and didn't have time to entertain me, I would take my friends and roam about the MGM lot where I watched *Tarzan* movies or whatever else was being filmed at the big studio where there was always something interesting happening.

It was a wonderful experience for a young boy. When the *Wizard of Oz* was released, I wasn't frightened for two reasons: I had seen so much of what was going on and was older then, and secondly, the very first day on the set I had seen all the Munchkins—there must have been four or five hundred of them. Several came over and talked with me in their outlandish costumes. I knew, of course, that they were adults even though I was bigger than many of them. One had a moustache with a little bit of egg on it and I knew that even adults got egg on their face at breakfast. One of the great sidelights was listening to the assistant directors giving instructions in several foreign languages because many of the Munchkins had been brought to America from Europe. It was like having my own private Disneyland.

We had a very close relationship as a family. I have a sister a few years older than I and there was none of the usual sibling rivalry. As a matter of fact, when I got into trouble she would protect me, trying to take the brunt of the punishment or would tell my mother, "He didn't mean to do it." Mom was the disciplinarian of the family. My father never raised his hand to me in his entire life. His way was to simply cut me off—not talk to me—which was worse. It nearly killed me when he did that. My mother, on the other hand, was not ashamed to go after me with a coat hanger or something similar. Nonetheless, we were a very loving family—a very stable family whose friends were people from vaudeville and from the Broadway stage.

Jack Haley, Jr. ☆ 129

There was an endless series of nannies and governesses. I don't recall having any major difficulties with them, but much thanks goes to our cook who, if she even suspected any sort of abuse toward my sister Gloria and me, would raise hell. In fact, my mother was talking the other night about one time when she and my father came home and the cook was chasing one of the governesses around the house with a cleaver in her hand—over some real or imagined abuse to me. There was one governess we had for a long time who was a marvelous lady and of whom I was quite fond, but we also had a couple of tyrants.

There were different cycles and different trends in governesses during the thirties and early forties. We had Teutonic governesses. I remember being dressed in lederhosen and walking all over Beverly Hills during the afternoon. At dinner my father would ask, "Why is he so flushed? Why is he so tired? Why is he falling asleep at dinner?" Then he found out I had been walking forty blocks a day and that was a lot on my little legs at the time. Fräulein, the governess, soon left our employ.

It was all a part of status—Beverly Hills style. I remember going to kids' parties where we would sit around together and gossip like agents or press agents. Every boy and girl in the film colony knew exactly what the actors or actresses—even directors—were doing and would exchange those tidbits with one another—mostly about his or her own parents. If Louella Parsons or Hedda Hopper had been smart, they would have sat in on some of those sessions and picked up more than a few "scoops."

Nannies also did their share of that sort of thing. There was a lot of one-upmanship among them. One got caught up in it as a spectator because they would show off their uniforms or hand-me-downs—used minks and things of that nature. A great deal of peer pressure was brought on the nannies. It was a caste system based on who their current employer was or their importance in the industry.

In spite of nannies and governesses, I was raised by my parents. They went out of their way to arrange for me to be with them if they went on the road; if my father was in New York to do a Broadway show, for instance, I went with them. I had that advantage over my sister who had spent a lot of time with my grandmother while Mother and Dad were out on tour, which they did a lot before I was born. It created difficulties for Gloria, and my parents, realizing that, made adjustments for me. I don't think Gloria developed a sense of home until she was in her preteens. Consequently I inherited a lot of extra affection that they perhaps felt guilty about denying her.

I went to private school both in Beverly Hills and New York. My God—all those schools. I recall when I was in the military service I was required from time to time to fill out forms listing my schools. It always involved extra pages to include them all. In grammar school I began my education at the Good Shepherd School in Beverly Hills, a Catholic school. Then another of those trendy situations occurred. There was a big rise in military schools. Status-conscious parents called them urbane. We all conformed. Later there was Saint John's, another Catholic school, in second and later seventh grade, where my classmates included the children of Don Ameche and Bing Crosby (his first family). Along the way I attended Professional Children's School in New York. I was never affected academically by being uprooted in my education. My marks were always excellent. School never seemed difficult for me. The traveling both excited and educated me. I attended Notre Dame High School in Van Nuys; then I found myself back in New York attending Mount Saint Michael's in the Bronx where I learned to play stickball. Later, I was probably the only kid living in Beverly Hills at the time who knew how to play stickball.

I took the Regent's exam for college and received a scholarship to Princeton University. The problem was, my father would have to change his residency in order for me to qualify, which was not part of his plans. I passed up the scholarship, entering Loyola in California where I graduated.

Until I discovered girls, I was mostly interested in motion pictures and show business in general. I was the first kid on our block with a 16mm camera and would get everybody together, write a screenplay, direct the picture, and go on location. I loved being behind the camera or putting on shows in our backyard. During one of my sojourns to New York, when I was in my early teens, we lived at the old Warwick Hotel next door to the Museum of Modern Art where I discovered silent films.

My father used to say I was "the only kid in Hollywood who knows who the hell John Bunny was." That was true. I was totally fascinated by Bunny films. I was so entranced by films that I persuaded my father to purchase a projector and we'd have kids over once a week to see *Frankenstein* or *King Kong* on our home screen. At the museum in New York I saw all the old Lon Chaney silent films and used to have nightmares from them—but I loved it.

So, as a young man I used any excuse to get backstage, on the set, to the radio station. The entire family would go down to watch Dad do his Sunday evening radio show. I had my own crowd at the studio because either Burns and Allen's children or somebody else would be around to keep me company.

I had friends both in and out of the business. Leslie Gargan, William Gargan's son, and Gary Crosby. Jay

Sandrich, who, incidentally, is one of the best directors in television today, lived right up the street. In New York I had other friends. Half the time I was in New York I grew up at night in the Stork Club where I met J. Edgar Hoover and Walter Winchell.

When I was at Fordham University back east for a spell, the guys were saying, "Hey, we have a celebrity here." They had heard that and had no idea it was me. I was just Jack "Somebody." They would either miss the name or ignore it. I never had difficulties at school because of who I was. Open and gregarious, I made friends rather easily. Whatever envy or cynicism was directed my way was more than compensated for by the nontheatrical kids being fascinated with my life. "What's Betty Grable like?" they would ask, or they wanted to know who were my father and mother's friends in Hollywood. I always had some good anecdotes and stories to tell them about Hollywood personalities. Sometimes I made up stories. Just being popular made one a minor celebrity in his own right.

All too often Hollywood children try to compete with their parents' enormous success and fall flat on their efforts. I never really wanted to do what my father did. Somehow he communicated the insecurity of being a performer to me very early in my life and that, combined with my fascination for being behind the camera, I think precluded any kind of "how-am-I-going-to-top-him" notions.

But I enjoyed some of the traditions of being a performer. I was enthralled with stories of vaudeville when George Burns would go on at great length or Fred Allen (who was my godfather) and Portland—and Jack Benny. These people would tell me their stories and I was awestruck. It was a life gone by.

Dad was as well known on Broadway as he was in

Hollywood. He did his last Broadway show in the late forties, *Inside U.S.A.* with Beatrice Lillie. Carl Reiner, Thelma Carpenter, and Herb Shreiner were also in the cast along with Jack Cassidy, who was always clowning around. I remember especially when he did *Show Time* with George Jessel and Kitty Carlisle because there was a young girl in the chorus who used to baby-sit me before she came to Hollywood and became a big star at MGM. Her name was June Allyson. My father was a very big star on Broadway. When he performed in *Higher and Higher* the entire show pivoted around him. In the movie, which starred Frank Sinatra, the whole thing was revamped to cash in on the Sinatra popularity. That's show business.

It was tougher, I am sure, on the Crosby boys. My father was a star. Bing was a superstar. Some of the Hollywood children I knew grew up very confused. Edward G. Robinson's son was an example of a child who couldn't cope with the celebrity stigma. Eddie came to me when I was doing my first film as a director and asked me to put his son in it. It was sad. Because Manny Robinson was an alcoholic nobody wanted to hire him, but I did. It was too late. The whole system had been more than he could handle.

Gary Crosby and I were always in some kind of trouble together. For instance, Pat O'Brien's daughter had a party and we went. Being kind of bored we started to snoop around the house. In one of the back rooms there was a lot of magic stuff that a magician, performing at the party, had spread out for his act. Gary and I screwed up all the tricks. When the man started to go through his act, nothing worked. Rabbits ran off. The pigeons were in the wrong place. It was a disaster and the poor man was near tears. Pat and my father knew the man was dying a terrible death up there and only two people were laughing— Gary and me. We were thrown out of the party by our ears.

Manny Robinson did something once at a party he gave. It was perhaps one of the two most elaborate children's parties I'd ever attended (the third being one I gave for maybe four or five hundred kids). The party took place at the Robinson estate back of Sunset Boulevard, up in the hills, with lots of acreage including horse corrals. The entire Police Circus had been hired for the occasion to entertain the offspring of Hollywood's most famous. Most of us had electric trains, but Manny was the only one of us who had tracks laid around the grounds with a train on which he could actually ride. This was before Walt Disney built one for his children.

Manny was a lonely, mixed-up child and was left alone often. He would talk to his friends, of whom I was one. His parents were not getting along and their opposite attitudes were transmitted to him in a negative way. In any event, to show you the extent and scope of this party, we were served a summons several weeks before the event. There was a knock on our door and a policeman was there with the paper in his hand. I remember my nurse taking me to the door and the policeman handing me this paper. I panicked—just carried on like crazy—from fear. I knew the police arrested people for being bad and I hadn't been *that* bad in my entire life. It turned out to be nothing more than an invitation to Manny's party, but I thought I was going to the slammer.

This was probably 1939 or 1940 and Eddie was at the peak of his popularity. I'm sure that Warner Brothers footed the bill for all of this. Finally the day of the party came. Parents went on ahead and the kids were picked up in paddy wagons. My sister was flirting with the cop who was riding in the back of the paddy wagon, so he let me ride outside on the steps with his arms around me while I watched these poor little fools inside shrieking and crying and carrying on. What trauma was laid on those kids for the sake of a clever device! On the outside, I'm sure I was

Jack Haley, Jr. ☆ 135

saying, "Yeah, you're going to jail and you'll never see your parents again."

At the party Gary and I immediately paired off. We couldn't have been more than eight or nine at the time. I know it was before World War II broke out. Manny said, "Come with me," so we followed him through the grounds. There was a big tent set up and the interior was done up like a western saloon with checkered tablecloths and sawdust on the floor—and a big long bar. It was an ice-cream bar where four or five guys dressed as western bartenders were dispensing sodas and other ice-cream confections. It was all quite festive. During a lull in the party Manny nudged Gary and me and said, "Watch this." There were huge open buckets of ice cream and he opened his fly and began peeing into all the ice cream. Gary and I exchanged glances of stark terror. His face was ashen white and I'm sure mine matched it. The two of us took off and probably beat the four-minute mile in getting the hell out of there.

Hollywood birthday parties came in all shapes and sizes in those days. We had a huge party at our house once and if I'm not mistaken the studio picked up the tab for that one, too. Hundreds of kids came, including the *Our Gang Comedy* group. I'd never met them before. This was sometime before Manny's debacle. It was one of my earliest experiences with all the birthday hoopla—organ-grinders, clowns, and an absolute sea of children, many of whom I did not even know. But that didn't matter. Often these big parties were just another excuse to get the parents together in a friendly atmosphere and had nothing to do with their offspring.

Atwater Kent, the famous radio inventor, often gave big parties and I remember one he gave for the children of celebrities. He loved show people and was always entertaining them. It was a real circus party—with an entire circus that had been playing in the Los Angeles area. The place was terraced and there were cages of real tigers and lions and down below a herd of elephants. That was for the children and the nannies. Inside all the parents were having drinks and enjoying their own gay times. Along with Butch Jenkins, Peggy Ann Garner, Elizabeth Taylor, and dozens of other kids, I was riding around on the elephants and caring less what my parents were doing. The ice cream was shaped in a tribute to *The Wizard of Oz*— huge ice-cream statues shaped like the Wicked Witch, the Tin Man, and so forth.

Although my father and Judy Garland did not hang out together, they felt a special affection for each other because he was in her first film, *Pigskin Parade*. And of course they costarred in *The Wizard of Oz*. When she and Mickey Rooney came through New York during the era of their films together and my dad was playing the Roxy, she liked to hang out around him. She liked his company. I remember he was quite hurt, however, that she never invited him to guest on her television series. I didn't meet Liza, who would later become my wife for a time, until she was fourteen.

I did do some entertaining. Whan I was about nine or ten I recall appearing as a guest on Fred Allen's radio show. It was a big event in my young life, standing up in front of a microphone with a large audience down in front of me. I later did some acting, but only as an excuse to get close to the cameras so I could see what went on behind them. Even much later, when I was a lieutenant in the air force, I made documentaries and newsreels in a unit that included George Stevens, Jr., and John Frankenheimer, who were only novices then, just as I was.

As a youngster, I suppose I was more intrigued with child stars than adults because adults in the business were always in and out of our home. Children like Shirley Temple, for instance, and Elizabeth Taylor, who sat across the table from me once and kept me entranced with those violet eyes of hers. Roddy McDowall, who was my age, was fascinating to me. I was a fan of kids my own age. I was far more interested in "Boy" than I was Tarzan.

I was in college when I first met Fred Astaire and the encounter absolutely knocked me out. Remember, I am the constant movie fan. But when you hang out at Bing Crosby's house a lot, you're not going to be overwhelmed by too many people. In high school I dated Maria Cooper, Barbara Warner, and Toni Wayne, so I got to meet their famous parents. Michael Wayne is my age. We went to college together. We hadn't known one another during the kiddie birthday days. Fred Astaire was not the usual movie star. He was never very social—so shy—but I loved him on the screen. Same thing with Gene Kelly (as an adult I would become his daughter's godfather).

Growing up with all these celebrity offspring and knowing many of their parents has been to my advantage, naturally, since many of us are in the same business. Having known one another so many years, we often do business without a lot of the formality strangers impose. There is a certain bond between children of major entertainers or major figures in this business. It is no different from kids who grow up in a small company town whose parents work for the same big company. In other words, I would be more comfortable with the child of another star than I would with somebody else.

I'm pleased that I am the son of a star, since I have chosen to be in this business. I am not surprised that so many of the celebrity offspring have been unable to kick the show business habit. Most of them start out wanting to be performers. When that doesn't work, they go down to the level that seemed, when they were children, less exciting—being behind a camera. I had a different attitude. I wanted to be behind the cameras. It is a dazzling industry. So I think the child of a star feels more impelled to pursue a glamorous profession that has enormous benefits if you are successful.

Many of us have taken advantage of having a famous parent in order to help ourselves professionally. Why not? It opens a lot of doors. You have to prove yourself, but I think you have to prove yourself in any business. There used to be an old saw that said, "If your father is an important performer or if your mother is an important performer—you better be terrific!"

The disadvantages are mostly emotional. You know, when you come from a broken home and multi-marriages and a crazy environment like Hollywood, there are many pitfalls. I have great admiration for those who were able to say, "I don't need this." Fred Astaire, Jr., for instance, is very happy with not being in show business.

I had a teen life that included the discovery of the opposite sex. I had early teen crushes but didn't start dating until my mid-teens. My first major romance was with Loretta Young's daughter, Judy Lewis. Judy and I have remained friends. My parents were not the type to sit down and give me the birds-and-bees story, but if one is an eavesdropper on adult conversations, one can pick up pretty quickly what it is all about—plus hanging around with the precocious children of other stars. It may not be your lifestyle, but the information rubs off. My older sister would sometimes steer me in the right direction when she sensed that I was off track about life. I picked up a lot on the run. When you're in your teens and hanging around chorus girls you'll learn quick enough. And I did. My first real experience at sex did not immediately change my life. There were no thunderclaps or flashes of lightning. She was older than I and it was rather poignant. I was raised as a gentleman and I've tried to maintain that in an environment where those qualities are not necessarily a prerequisite for getting along with young ladies. I must say, however, that my first experience left me with a soft spot in my heart for dancers.

God has been very good to me. I always happened to be at the right place at the right time and things have turned out so well. I cannot say that nothing in my childhood ever disappointed me. I wasn't always in the school of my choice and there were some lonely nights when I would wish I was doing something else, but on the whole, I had a very happy childhood, a very adventuresome childhood.

I had freedom, but not financial freedom as some might think. My parents kept strict reins on money that went into my jeans. It wasn't only my father. Gary Crosby didn't have a lot of spending money either. That, in a sense, was good, because we had to do extra errands and other chores to get extra spending money for the movies or whatever it was we wanted. There were some crazy fun times. It was great sneaking into a studio for the first time. Bob Wagner and I used to go over the back fence at Fox. It was more fun than going in the front gate. Little did I know that someday he would have a production company and be a big star. Those studio cops were not stupid. They didn't care who the hell you were if you sneaked in. We would always get rattled when we were grabbed up by the scruff of the neck and taken into the offices. Somebody would ask, "Where did you come through?" We were too frightened to lie and they would deliberately take us to the other end of the studio and put us out. We would be several miles from where we had left our bikes, so the real punishment was the walk back.

It was all great fun. I'm relatively stable, disciplined, and able to have a good time. Success was not just handed to me. I went on many interviews for jobs I didn't get. A good observer, I wasn't ever temperamental. Mine was more of a neighborhood upbringing than that of a movie star's kid.

Pamela Chase (Diana's sister, a prominent Hollywood screenwriter and novelist), Mary Herbert (Pamela and Diana's stepmother), F. Hugh Herbert, and teenaged Diana Herbert at Los Angeles Airport, December 24, 1949.

Courtesy of Diana Markes

9

Diana Markes

L ike most other people, I've always had trouble distinguishing between Hugh Herbert, the funny movie actor, and F. Hugh Herbert, the playwright and screenwriter who gave us Clifton Webb as Mr. Belvedere in *Sitting Pretty*—who helped Maggie McNamara make film history with the use of the word *virgin* in *The Moon Is Blue*.

Diana Markes is the daughter of playwright F. Hugh Herbert. She is remarkably talented and candid. She is the sort of woman whom virile men refer to as "my kind of broad," a genuine, gutsy, "I-can-do-it-myself" female handling the nuclear society with all the aplomb of "a kid poking a match down the gas tank." If it happens—so what, as long as it makes a big bang.

I liked her immensely and I think hers is a tender, tragic yet often comedic story. She is one of Hollywood's Children from an era when motion-picture celebrities didn't have children. She epitomizes one facet of the Hollywood diamond that has seldom been revealed to the public.

I should preface this by explaining who I am—nobody would recognize the name. My father was F. *Hugh* Herbert. I say the "Hugh" loudly because my early childhood was spent defending the parting of the name on the left. All through school the boys used to say "F you"; even the telephone operators got it mixed up. He was a writer, playwright, a dreamer.

He was best known for his plays, tremendously successful on Broadway, that were made into highly successful movies—*The Moon Is Blue, Kiss and Tell*—and one of his first films, *Sitting Pretty,* which introduced the world to the irascible sophisticate, Mr. Belvedere, so captivatingly brought to life in the person of Clifton Webb. Daddy was known for his "firsts." *The Moon Is Blue* introduced the word *virgin* to the screen; *Kiss and Tell* thrilled the world with Shirley Temple's first screen kiss; and *Sitting Pretty* said more of what everybody had wanted to do to bratty kids—but held back.

My mother was his secretary—his first wife. He later married another of his secretaries. When my mother met my father she was a young girl of seventeen or eighteen who never should have gotten married—certainly not to my father. Mother was from Texas, a beauty. Dad was a shy man, not very physically attractive, although he had many friends. I believe he was actually quite backward with women. My mother was unhappy in the marriage from the very beginning and so my early childhood memories are of nothing but fights and different bedrooms. It wasn't a good marriage. When my sister and I were five and six and Mother decided to leave my father and go on her own, he said, "I don't know if I can live by myself. What shall I do? I'm almost helpless."

Mother quite practically said, "Why don't you marry your secretary?"

"Marry?"

"Yes, marry. She's perfect for you—and who would know better than I?" He married his secretary and that marriage was an excellent one.

Mother was an earth person. She could do anything she wanted to do—a Taurus on the cusp of Gemini. Quite an athlete, she was a championship bowler. I was so proud when she won the Los Angeles Times Bowling Tournament one year. My sister and I had our pictures taken with Mother as they presented her the prize—a new car. They pushed a microphone in front of my face and asked what I thought of the whole affair. I said, "Yes, it's fine, but I think the color of the car is ugly." Everybody broke up and I gave my first public performance as a comedienne. I loved the roar of laughter and thought to myself, I want to do that some more. I really like that.

When mother remarried, she married a man much younger than herself and she, too, had a marvelous second marriage. I never understood about repeating patterns, but I have repeated my mother's pattern in almost every phase of my life. I tend to go for men considerably younger than myself, I'm very independent, I love mothering, but I also love my sexuality. I recognize so much about my mother now that I am a mother myself. She was a very sexual person and her conflict—between motherhood and sexuality—is one we now know was not unique to her generation.

Mother died about thirteen years ago and my father twenty years ago, never knowing that he was a grandfather-to-be. It is a shame because he wanted a grandchild so badly.

I was born in Hollywood Hospital—the first baby born in Los Angeles on Christmas Day 1928, one minute into the new day. It was in the papers and the fact that my father was a film writer had nothing to do with it—it was my accomplishment for having come out, upstaging my father.

I went to many, many schools. Because of the divorce my mother wanted to get as far away from my father as she could—or so it seemed. She was a nomad, moving from community to community in rapid succession, so I attended fifteen or sixteen schools in the growing-up process—public schools on "the other side of the hill." The celebrity community is divided today between the Hollywood/Beverly Hills side of the Santa Monica Mountains and the hill corridor on the San Fernando Valley side where I now live. I was born on the "south side" of the mountains.

We lived in a small house on Hayworth Avenue very near where CBS Television City is now located at Fairfax and Beverly Boulevard. Fairfax was only a dirt road into Beverly Hills when I was a little girl, dotted by nothing more than bungalows. The La Brea Tar Pits was my playground. I was always into some sort of mischief which often brought discipline from my mother.

When Mother punished me for something, she used the most serious weapon a mother can use—holding back her approval and love. I remember that!

I have a selective memory, however, remembering only what I want to. My sister, on the other hand, remembers everything. I used to create an image of my earliest times for my former husband who would look at me sternly and say, "Don't tell me that. You had a terrible childhood. Your sister told me all about it." I would be shocked. How could he tell me I had a terrible childhood? I was there—he wasn't. But my sister was probably right, in spite of the fact I still think I had a wonderful childhood.

Before my mother and father divorced when I was six, I remember a lot of screaming and yelling between them. My mother moved out of "their" bedroom into one of her own upstairs, apart from my father. I remember muffled arguments and the sounds of doors slamming at all hours of the night and my father storming down the stairs in the morning, slamming the front door behind him as he departed for the studio, with no thought of saying to us, "It's OK, kids." Each time he left, I thought it would be the last I'd ever see him.

Once, when my father was married to my stepmother, I thought I'd have to go through that all over again. They were having an argument of some sort over a bridge game. Suddenly my father jumped up from the table and said, "That's it! That's it! I've had it! I'm leaving!" Whereupon he flung himself out the door, while my sister and I both burst into tears, throwing ourselves on our stepmother who was totally bewildered. My father walked back into the house a few minutes later very casually and seeing all the hysteria asked, "Wha— what happened?" It was beyond explaining. I blurted out, "Where did you go?"

"Nowhere—just to put the car away." His action evoked a bad memory from the past when he used to do just that very thing—and meant it. It triggered a tremendous feeling of loss. I asked him never to do that again.

I'll never forget the divorce between my mother and dad. Mother called me into the bedroom. I remember Mother in bed a lot. She slept late; to me, that's always been a sin, even though it is luxurious. Mother didn't tell my sister because it was always assumed she was too young to understand. Since I was older, I would have to explain it to her. In Ancient Greece, they killed the bearer of such gross news. Mother said, "Your father and I are going to get a divorce."

"What does that mean?"

"It means we are going to move out of this house." I didn't like that idea. I loved the house we were living in. It was my security. It was the house in which all my dreams happened. Even to this day I relate to that house, whatever the dream is, whoever the characters are. My mother related the facts rather coldly and unemotionally: "Your father and I don't love each other anymore. That's what all the screaming has been about. We're going to divorce and you'll be coming to live with me."

After she had broken the ice, my father took me into the study, which was a very masculine room. He cried and said, "Your mother doesn't love me anymore." He proceeded to tell me some other things that probably would have been better left unsaid. "Your mother never wanted to have you. I'm the one who wanted you. She wanted an abortion. When she became pregnant again with your sister, she didn't want her either. I forced her to bear you both and now she's leaving me and she's taking both of you away from me." That broke my heart and I cried inside for days and weeks.

My father fought for us. We went through two very notorious court battles. It was a front-page scandal. It was only as an adult that I knew the whole story. The newspapers detailed every sordid and seamy scrap of evidence my parents threw at each other. All those horrible headlines and pictures of us in court and being hustled down corridors—and always the quotes from Mother on the witness stand defending herself against charges of being an unfit mother. Years later, the pattern was repeated. My ex-husband took me to court for custody of our children and charged me as unfit. He lost, just as my father did. But in 1935, it was much more sensational reading.

We were awarded to my mother which, in those days, was automatic. We induced my father into court several times because we wanted to live with him, but each time the court refused him. I remember the judge whose name was Albert Pianesso. I told him, and my sister hasn't forgiven me for it (she didn't know what she wanted at the time and I spoke for both of us), "We *want* to live with our father."

On his way from chambers after a recess, His Honor mentioned to someone in the hallway, "I have a very difficult thing to do today—I have to take two little girls away from their mother and give them to their father." He promptly went into the courtroom and continued the custody with Mother. What happened between the corridor and the bench is something I will never know, but he did an absolute turnabout. I suppose he just couldn't resist tradition—the mother *always* got the kids.

It would be five or six years before I could live with my father again. In the interim we lived all over the Los Angeles basin, all of which served me well—both then and now. It taught me how to get along with people instantly—how to fit in and evaluate where *I* wanted to be. I would walk into my new school, pick the group of people I wanted to be with, and I would fit in with them. I immediately ran for a school office—and was usually elected. I'd join the drama club because that was the quickest way to become known. I picked out the boy of my choice and got him. So I made changing schools become an experience to serve my needs. I never counted on tomorrow simply because I didn't know where and what tomorrow would be.

My sister and I are admittedly as different as night and day. We have both agreed that if we were not related we wouldn't even be friends, although now we are the closest of friends, talking on the phone three or four times a day. She has a very good analogy of the two of us. "Diana," she said, "if you and I walk into a crowded room you will look around and say, 'Who is here who is going to love me and whom am I going to love?' I will look around and say, 'I wonder who's going to steal my purse.' " It is true. She is suspicious of people and of Hollywood—yet a highly respected, talented, professional writer who will one day win an Academy Award. Her novel *Split Ends* was very well received, and she is now already in the middle of her second and third novels—simultaneously. An excellent comedy writer, she has written for *All in the Family* and *Maude* regularly.

Growing up we were extremely close. Since she was younger, I absolutely dominated her early life. I believe she still has an enormous amount of hate for me (whether she knows it or not). Fortunately we can deal with it. It comes out and I accept it—I earned it.

I tried to be her mother. Even after I was grown, living in New York and running my own affairs, when she came to live with me, after her divorce, I picked up where I left off in childhood—took the role of her mother and wouldn't even let her go out of the house in clothes *she* had selected. It was a constant "Where are you going? Who are you going to be with? You can't leave here!"

She had to put me in my place. "I am *me*," she told me firmly. "You're not my mother." That's all changed now. A total role reversal. She is *my* mother; she is the one who goes "Cluck, cluck, cluck" and "tsk, tsk, tsk!" I seek her approval and want her to not find my choices wrong.

For instance, I recently had a face-lift. She is the happily married woman and is happy just the way she is. She reacted to my surgery with, "I know. I know. You're going to look like my daughter. I'm perfectly well prepared for that."

Yes, there is a lot of my mother in me. I see some of the innate dissatisfaction and searching for one's self. I remember the pulling and tugging within me on weekends when I lived with Mother. Sunday nights were a painful experience and I had a real identity crisis over visitation. A wave of anguish and pain and separation came over me—having to leave my father and go home to my mother. It was the change that was hard; because on Friday when I was going to go visit Dad, I would feel the same anguish. I just didn't want to be disturbed—wanted to stay in my nest and be left alone. I would ask God in my prayers: "Why do I have to change and go for half a vacation here and half there?"

That has been visited upon my children, too. I have seen it happen—when they would have to go and leave me and visit their father on weekends. Thank God it doesn't happen anymore. If they don't choose to go, they don't; more often than not, now, they don't. There's a terrible backlash to that—I don't ever get to be alone anymore. I don't have those blessed weekends when I didn't have to prepare a meal if I didn't want to. It destroyed a very good relationship I had going with an extremely nice guy. We just didn't have privacy anymore—and the kids always come first. That's the way it is.

I learned about film studios (my children have, too) early on. My sister and I often visited my father around the studios and I loved the sound stages—still do. He worked everywhere: Universal, Fox, Warner Brothers—though most of his movies were at Fox. He would have us to lunch at the commissary or on the set—all of which made me want to be an actress, made me want to be in the business, to be part of it. To this day when I walk onto a sound stage I'm engulfed with the nostalgic smells and sounds that take me back to when I was a little girl—and the thrill of this wonderful world in which my father was a king. I can almost feel him by my side at those times.

I am starstruck and have always been. Nevertheless, I was jealous of anyone who achieved what I wanted so much to achieve. Because of that, I had no idols. I was horrified at the thought of collecting autographs. It meant they had made it and I had not. One of my peak embarrassments and angers was when my father was working on a film, *That Certain Age,* which he wrote for Deanna Durbin who was the rage at the time. He had also written her big movie *100 Men and a Girl,* in which she costarred with symphony conductor Leopold Stokowski.

Daddy just assumed that my sister and I wanted to meet Deanna and had us to lunch at the commissary when he knew she would be there. I loved the old Universal commissary. It was a thrilling place with its screened porch and the sound of the screen door slamming as people came in and out—it was actually nothing more than hamburgers and cellophane wrapped sandwiches, but it was excitement. We were sitting munching hamburgers with Cokes when Dad said, "Oh, there's Deanna—I'll get her autograph for you."

I almost choked on my food and sputtered out, "Oh, no! Daddy, no!" He didn't even hear me and turned to where she sat down behind us, stood up, and said, "Deanna, I'd like you to meet my daughters Diana and Pamela. They'd like to have your autograph." I was absolutely livid and mortified. Humiliated! I did *not* want her autograph. I didn't want *her* stardom. I did not want *her* fame. I did not even want to know her. She was there and I wasn't and I resented it. To this day, asking a star friend for his or her autograph for another friend or a child is almost impossible for me. Of course, I love to give mine when somebody asks me—I loved those wonderful people outside the Broadway stage doors in New York wanting autographs. My father was a king, so I wanted to be the crown princess!

I *wanted* to be those things, but I was always filled

with uncertainties. When I was about thirteen or so I went with my sister one weekend to visit my father and step-mother—he *had* married his secretary at my mother's suggestion. I always expressed a desire to live with my father and stepmother on these weekly sojourns. This particular weekend I was going through my litany about how much I wanted to live in *my* old home, using Pamela as a sounding board. We were interrupted by my stepmother, who came upstairs with my father to our room and said, "You don't have to go home—either of you."

I didn't understand. "What do you mean?"

She smiled warmly and said, "Your mother has agreed to let you stay here—permanently."

We didn't see our mother again for years—throughout our teens and adolescence—the really important years when a girl needs a relationship with her mother. She made the decision without consulting us in any way. She wanted to get married. The man who would become my stepfather wanted to travel and didn't want children. Mother's choice turned out to be quite profitable for her and her new husband; before she gave us up, my father made a large settlement of money on her. We were purchased from our mother for a price. I went through school and young adulthood without seeing my mother and bore the guilt of being sold to my father. Not that he didn't want me—my God, the man would have sold his soul to have us live with him—it was just my not understanding my mother or what motivated her. That didn't come for many years.

I knew my mother existed, even though she stopped all communication and never once contacted us. Never wrote a letter. A couple of Christmases she brought a box of gifts and left them on the doorstep and we'd open them up and make fun of what she had brought us—she didn't know us and they were not what a mother would buy for a daughter. It was sad, our laughter. We were laughing at a mother who didn't even know who we were, actually.

I made a commitment to Mary, my stepmother. She became my mother—I even called her "Mother." We just eliminated our real mother from our lives. Pamela was unhappy, because once again she had been dragged (actually by me) into all these life changes. I had chosen for her and she resented it.

We lived in luxury with my father, but never had money of our own. I received one-dollar-a-week allowance—and it was only $1.50 after I entered college. But I didn't need money. Anything I wanted, I got. My father was generous with gifts all his life. When he finished *Sitting Pretty,* which was such a smash-hit film, he purchased Pam and me a new maroon 1948 Plymouth. It was gorgeous. We promptly named it "Mr. Belvedere," which was the character played by Clifton Webb in the film.

I was a freshman at UCLA. Although Pam was not yet in college, we still had to share the car. Dad allowed us five dollars a week between us for gasoline. He gave us the car on the condition that if one of us left home first, the other would automatically own the car outright. When I went to New York to work in the theater, Pam received the car. I thought that was grossly unfair, but Dad said it was his money and he would dispose of it as he chose. That car meant a lot to me, but my career meant more. I opted for the stage and gave up the freeways to my sister.

My parents' divorce presented a similar situation. Daddy kept the house, which was totally unheard of at that time. Going back there was going back to the womb for me. We moved from West Hollywood to Belair in one swift transition—from the little bungalow in a dumpy little area to a fabulous mansion. It was like instant stardom and I loved it. My life changed. Daddy was on a first-name basis with the elite of Hollywood. He was a true success. I remember he was very fond of Shirley Temple and because of their close association in pictures and on a personal level, we were invited to her wedding to John Agar. It was a real celebrity event and my first big wedding. What a gala. Everybody in Hollywood was there. I've never seen so many flowers. John Agar was an eight-by-ten glossy, the likes of which you have never seen—absolutely a beautiful specimen of manhood. It was not to be a good marriage, however.

I was about fourteen or fifteen and felt awkward. Girls my age were not built the way they are today and what we had was de-emphasized. If you had a waist your mother arranged it so that the dress was either too low or too high, and if you had breasts they were disguised in some manner. The styles were terrible and I never thought I looked pretty.

The wedding was held at a Wilshire Boulevard Church and then the reception at the Shirley Temple estate. Shirley's playhouse was really a huge guesthouse, the main parlor of which had been transformed into a gift display room for the wedding gifts. The place was like Saks, Robinson's, Bergdorf-Goodman—you name it—all dumped into one room. I couldn't imagine how any one person, not much older than myself, could use all that in her whole lifetime. I mean, how many salad bowls did she need? How many silver service spoons? I've never seen so much of the same thing. Of course, I was overcome and thrilled by it. With all my resentment of the starlike goddesses, I never resented Shirley Temple at all. She was the exception. I thought she was quite divine.

I was pleased to see that people got married young. Shirley's wedding was interesting from that point of view because I was a very sexual person who discovered early needs and had pretty much surmised that marriage was supposed to precede sex. I was always a sexual creature (as was my mother). The forbidden subject—masturbation—was a function I was aware of from the age of four. I never had sexual inhibitions as a child.

I played with everything that could be played with and didn't think it was wrong. Nobody ever suspected I was into sexual feelings, so nobody ever told me I shouldn't. In nursery school I would stay in from recess with a boy who had been punished and couldn't go out with the rest of the class—in order to keep him company and feel the warmth of his body next to mine. I kissed all the boys and they kissed me. I loved kissing them back.

The girls hated me. They would taunt me on the playground with things like, "You think you're so good because the boys love you."

I'd say, "Yes, you're right. I do." The boys did love me and I loved them back. I used to organize spin-the-bottle games in grammar school (after class). I'd invite all the boys over and play that game with them. When I was living with my mother in Pacific Palisades, she had taken a large vacant lot next to the house and made it into a badminton court, surfacing it in gravel. I would mark off areas in the gravel—playing house. I would draw a big bedroom and bathroom and make the boys go into the bedroom and bathroom with me—from my earliest memories I did that sort of thing.

I was seriously necking from the age of twelve and would have had sexual intercourse if my father had not nipped one of my big romances in the bud. We were already into oral sex. Dad simply refused to allow me to see the young man again—he sensed we were too serious about each other.

I turned being born on Christmas Day into a positive thing, so I wouldn't feel cheated. I used to say that everybody had a party on my birthday. Because of it, I was cut off the radio one night. I was a guest on the Jack Eigen Show from the Copacabana—it was in the lounge and all the performers would stop by to plug their acts. I was a frequent guest because I loved to talk and Jack was a personal friend. One night, on his show, we were talking about birthdays and how people celebrated them. I said, "Well, everybody celebrates two birthdays on Christmas—mine and Jesus Christ's!" I might as well have raped the pope. We were immediately cut off the air and replaced by some canned music. The sponsor blew it and I was never allowed back on that show. So much for unintended sacrilege.

I was an overnight Broadway star—in a sense. I had almost completed my second year at UCLA when I had the opportunity to go to New York to appear in my father's play, *The Moon Is Blue,* replacing June Lockhart. Afterward I toured with the play, and although I didn't know it at the time, I wouldn't be coming back home. But how many girls who aspire to acting can go to New York and start at the top? That will spoil you for any other life—forever. I got the part because of my father. I'm not ashamed of that. The attendance was beginning to fall off and the producers felt if the playwright's daughter had the lead it might keep the play going for eight weeks, maybe, instead of six. It had publicity value and I was thrilled to have that kind of experience.

On the road, in summer stock, in Chicago I fell madly in love with Conrad Nagel—desperately, madly in love. He was the first of my father figures. Then the play closed and I was out of work—and out of love. It didn't seem to matter that I was F. Hugh Herbert's daughter anymore. As a matter of fact, it was a hindrance in many ways. People were saying, "What the hell—this rich kid is just playing around, trying to take food out of the mouths of the real working actors." It was tough. I had to work twice as hard as the next person to get the job—and even harder if I was employed. I hung in, supported myself from the very beginning, and never asked for support from home.

My reunion with my mother was another giant trauma in my life. I was in New York working in and around Broadway when I received a letter from Pamela. I picked up the mail on my way to an interview and read it on the Madison Avenue bus. As I read her letter, I started to cry and it became so embarrassing I had to get off before my stop. In the letter she described finding our mother and confronting her after all these years. Through friends, she discovered Mother had an upholstery shop in the west end of Los Angeles and she simply walked into the shop one day. They hadn't seen each other in ten years. Mother walked up to my sister, who was in her early twenties, and said, "Is there anything I can do for you?" My sister just stood there until recognition came and there was a beautiful, tearful reunion.

I couldn't wait to see my mother. All the fears, guilt, petty hatreds—all went out the window. She was my mother and I wanted to see her. Since I couldn't get away immediately, we corresponded with each other and it was like reading a chapter out of one's life that was missing from the book.

Returning to California, my sister arranged for me to meet Mother at lunch in a Mexican restaurant because Mom loved Mexican food. She was terrific. I was so anxious to display my maturity and I wanted to just take out all of my life and say, "Look what you missed."

I had a fabulous relationship with her for the rest of her life and she was a wonderful grandmother to my children. She made up, with my kids, for all the nonmothering of me. She had been unable to give me that kind of love simply because she had been too young to cope. Those years of absence had helped me to cut the cord and be a person. I didn't have to hate her anymore.

I was my mother's daughter after all. Just like her first marriage, my marriage was also doomed. But I didn't carry tremendous guilt when my marriage failed. I didn't say to myself, "My God, what am I doing to my children?" I took all of them to a therapist whether they needed it or not—which turned out to be of great benefit to them. They were allowed to express their feelings of hate, anger, and hostility—I was never allowed such privileges. My kids get angry with me. So what? Have at it, get it all out. I don't want them harboring all that crap I did for years. My kids are pleased with me—and that is certainly a reversal of my feelings at their ages.

I've tried to make it different for them. My mother and father did not like each other. I was cut off from my mother for years and could never mention her name in my father's house.

I went through EST—loved it. I got a great deal from that experience. It is something I can always use—not like algebra, which is a total waste. I remember when I started EST the guy was standing up in front of us—about two hundred and fifty in my class I think—and he said, "Look, everything I'm going to tell you, you already know." It was true. I was learning to be responsible for my own actions—and forever on, I wouldn't have to feel guilty or blame somebody else for what happened to me. And it enabled me to pass on my freedom to my children.

In the era in which I grew up, you weren't supposed to tell your daughter she was pretty, because she would get "stuck up." You weren't supposed to tell your son that he did something nice. Compliments were kept to a minimum. It was the era—not just my parents. I would, if I could, go back and have them build up my ego more as a child. It has taken me a long time for me to like me. Why were all those years wasted? I spend more time telling my girls and boys how beautiful they are and how accomplished and smart and clever they are—and showing it off to everybody. I had those talents and abilities, too, but they were squashed. I resent that.

I would have liked to change my father's attitude about women—he was a chauvinist who believed that women were mothers and stayed home and if they had a career it was a toy or game and would be over soon and they'd go back to the real life of being a mother. He could have, because of his financial situation, encouraged me to go to any university in the world, but he didn't. He deemphasized education for us girls—so completely. With my children it is not a question of whether they'll go to college—it is a question of when and where.

In spite of all this I would not alter myself personally. Everything happened because it happened—where I am today is result of all that—even if I did have to go through EST and a few other things. I wouldn't have done that if my early life hadn't been structured as it was and I wouldn't have my head in the same place it is now. So, no changes—not really.

The advantages of being the child of a celebrity— there were the open doors, before my father died and when his name meant something. People loved him. I never heard anyone in Hollywood badmouth him. As one of the first presidents of the Writers Guild of America West, he helped bring recognition to writers. Helped bring them out of the studio cubicles to the recognition they deserved. He is partly responsible for the freedoms Hollywood writers have today. Most of them don't know that; some of the younger ones were probably barely born when he died, so the advantage of my being a Hollywood

Child was having doors opened and being proud that F. Hugh Herbert was *my* father.

And the disadvantages—skepticism in the industry that there could be any talent left over for me. People thought I was a rich girl messing around, rather than a serious actress looking for parts. I didn't get to the top—maybe I didn't try hard enough. I'm a good actress. Maybe I'm satisfied that *I* know that, even if the world doesn't. I don't know.

Perry Anthony poses for a school picture at one of the numerous military schools he attended as a youngster. The smile belies his unhappiness at the time.

Courtesy of Mamie Van Doren

Mamie Van Doren, Perry Anthony's mother

10

Perry Anthony

Perry's parents are band leader Ray Anthony and sex symbol/actress Mamie Van Doren. With a handsome father who has remained a bachelor since his divorce from Mamie many, many years ago—and who has a reputation for being quite the swinger—and a gorgeous blonde mother, well known for her lovers on *and* off screen, it is an irony that Perry, now in his mid-twenties, attends a strict religious college, has deep Christian convictions, and is totally opposed to premarital sex of any kind.

One's admiration for Mamie Van Doren grows listening to her son Perry unravel the threads of his life—the child of celebrities. His mother, he avows, has been with him all the way, never wavering in her support both emotionally and financially. It is obvious that he adores her—and without question, she worships him. His relationship with his father can only be described as nonexistent. "My father has disinherited me and doesn't even speak to me," the young man said, choking with emotion as he told the story that certainly had to be painful. "I would just like to get all of this out and maybe then I can feel better about the whole thing." And that's just what he did—totally un-abashed—hanging on to little slivers of hope that he has for the future where his father is concerned.

My life has been a sequel of struggles. My parents were divorced sometime between my third and fifth year. I have practically no recollection of my mother and father living together. I've been a very lonely child all my life. Mom was gone most of the time because she had to work. There were some nice neighbors who sometimes looked after me. We had maids, but they weren't very reliable. They're OK for taking care of the house, but not children. That's what parents are for. Sometimes it just can't be helped. Somebody has to make a living.

I had very few pals or playmates. Just kids who lived in the neighborhood—sometimes. I've never had anything that could be reasonably called a father/son relationship with my dad. If I saw him every six months while I was growing up it was something special—and he rarely ever called. I used to think he was Santa Claus because he bought me a ton of gifts on Christmas. That was about it. In order to get attention I often broke the toys he sent. Once I totally dismantled a four-hundred-dollar nickel-odeon my father bought me. He wasn't even angry. He replaced it with another expensive plaything.

Mom was there when I needed her and spent as much time as she could with me. I lived a great part of my youth with her parents. No matter where she worked, she phoned to see if I was all right and if I needed anything. Although I don't recall being on movie sets with her, she did take me along when she worked in summer stock and I remember being with her when she filmed some Aqua

Velva television commercials. That was an ego thing for me—for a little kid, it was something special.

My dad was much more popular then than he is now. Once in a great while I would spend some time with him. Most of those memories are tainted by some ridiculous act of his. I always thought he was ashamed of me, but couldn't figure out why. I remember distinctly one such incident when he refused to give me my suitcase. I was staying at a hotel with his singing girls, The Book Ends, and only had minimal clothing with me. I guess he thought it was some kind of funny joke not to let me have my clothing—part of his strange sense of humor. I had a good time anyway because The Book Ends always made me feel wanted.

Dad had his methods of administering discipline. He never hit me. We used to wrestle, but he stopped when I started winning. He has an obsession against losing at anything. One time I got a D in handwriting and he made me write a sentence over and over and over for three straight days. My handwriting didn't improve one bit. On the other hand, as an incentive to getting good grades, he once offered fifty dollars for an A and twenty-five dollars for a B. That was a snap. I almost always made good grades academically even though I never put too much effort into doing it. Things just came to me. I never cared much if the grades were good or not.

When I was a little kid, my father was just like a god in my eyes. I wanted so much to impress him and make him proud of me. Yet, nothing I ever did seemed to please him. I honestly do not know why, because I sure tried.

He doesn't seem to have made lasting relationships with women either—except for his mother. After my mother divorced him, he never remarried. I would hear and read about the various women in his life.

Dad is not only a soloist with his trumpet on the bandstand, but just as much a soloist off the bandstand. He still looks like a young man. Always into himself, he keeps his body trim for the suits he has custom-tailored, and runs around in a big Mercedes being Mr. Ray Anthony. Yet he didn't want to pay my tuition in college. Bitter? Yes, but I have been hurting for my father's love all my life.

Mom has been my chief support. In the divorce decree my dad was ordered to pay monthly child support. There were a few times when he cut off the checks. Mom threatened to take him back to court. He got around that by playing on my love and emotions. Once he bought me a car and I talked Mom out of going back to court. He eventually resumed the support payments.

When I was nine years old I went to live with my mother's parents in Azusa, California where I was enrolled in a daytime military academy. I appreciated coming back to a home every day after school. I knew kids who boarded and they mostly looked like they'd just been left off and forgotten. It also frightened me because I thought maybe someday that might happen to me. Thanks to my mother, it never did.

Grandma was a great substitute mother. She and Grandpa showered me with love and affection. I think they knew how lonely I was. My grandma and I were very close. She often took me into Los Angeles and we'd shop at all the stalls in the Farmer's Market. Those were wonderful times. My grandma and grandpa were Lutherans and very moralistic. Although I am now a Christian, at that time I wasn't religious. But when my grandparents went to church, I went along with them. Later, a growing faith in God held me together during some hectic times. Times when I felt so lonely and despondent that I considered suicide.

Military school was difficult for me. It was based on hard discipline, something I hadn't had much of in my life. Because of that, to this day I still call everybody "sir" and "ma'am." I learned about politics for the first time. One boy's mother worked in the school administration offices. He got promotions with regularity. On the "outs" with the commandant, I got demoted. One teacher stopped my promotion in rank on five different occasions simply because I had talked in class. It wasn't happening to other students and I often wondered if it was because they knew who my parents were. I was drummed out of my rank when I lost my position in the platoon—before the entire battalion. My stripes were ripped off as if I were in the French foreign legion.

After some long discussions with my mother and grandma, I left military school—with no little amount of joy. I was then enrolled in sixth grade at another school in Azusa.

Mom got married again, this time to the baseball pitcher, Lee Meyers. He was young and I liked him. A nice guy and really like a friend to me. And a father. I went to baseball games and all the things I had supposed a father would do with his son. He was young, but he really tried. He taught me a lot of things and nobody was more distraught than I when he was killed in a tragic accident.

I was about thirteen or so. Drugs would have been an easy out, but I'd once found a balloon filled with white powder hidden in a fire hydrant receptacle in an apartment building we were visiting. It tasted horrible, so I spit it out and threw the balloon away. It had no effect on me—except that when I learned it was probably heroin, I knew drugs were not for me.

While Mom and Lee were married, I lived with them first in Newport News, Virginia, where he was pitching for the local team and later at Newport Beach when we moved back to the West Coast. When they broke up, I went back to Azusa to live with Grandma again. Mom came with me for a while. It was great to be with her and Grandma at the same time. But she had her career and was soon back on the road again. It was during the stay with Grandma that Mom got interested in antiques. That led to the great antique business she opened at Newport Beach—she always had a good business head.

In Azusa we lived in an area where almost nobody spoke English—only Spanish. Spanish-speaking people tend to be clannish and I was an outsider. Not understanding the language, I was often the target of both verbal and physical abuse. I was "rich."

The second school I attended in Azusa was a very conservative establishment. There could have been more pressure put on me there. Conservative people have their own impressions of what show people are like. Fortunately the principal, also an entertainer and a big fan of Mom's, took that into consideration. Because of him, I entered the school without having to take the entrance exams. Some things can be said for celebrity—it opens doors.

At Western Christian I took up trumpet—hoping it might create a common bond between my father and me. I became part of the scene there. I was in. I was a teenager, accepted by my peers. What a great time I was having: got my driver's license and started playing trumpet! I was into things for the first time in my life that made me feel good as a person. I started out playing third chair and moved up rapidly as a member of the band.

I played church music, of course. My first trumpet solo was "Near the Cross." My first year I took a blue ribbon in competition at one of the interschool festivals. I felt great.

My father's recordings were a mainstay for me. I listened to everything he ever recorded and knew every phrase and pause in his charts. Actually, I only knew him through his music, because I rarely saw him. Mom would come home from time to time and spend two or three weeks with me and we'd have great times together. She always wanted me to enjoy myself. I cannot say enough for the encouragement she gave me when she knew my heart was breaking because Dad ignored me most of the time.

The times we did spend together are ones I remember vividly. Once he had me up to Las Vegas where he was playing with his band at the Frontier Hotel. I was so anxious to see him I took an early flight. When I walked into his rehearsal he stopped everything, looked at his watch, and yelled across the room at me: "You're not supposed to be here yet!" I was totally embarrassed in front of the band and everybody else there. He never apologized. He has never ever apologized to me for that or anything else.

There were other such experiences. When I graduated from eighth grade at Western Christian I played a solo—"The Sound of Music"—on my trumpet. Dad was there and complimented me. It was one of the happiest moments of my life. Later on, Mom went to Vietnam to entertain the troops. It was a rough trip for her. Suffering from dehydration and exhaustion, she was transferred to a hospital in Hawaii. As it happened, my father's band was playing at the Royal Hawaiian Hotel on Waikiki Beach. I went over to see Mom and on my arrival Dad greeted me with, "You wouldn't be here if your mother wasn't in the hospital."

In spite of the not-so-warm reception from him I had a great time. The Book Ends were there and I stayed with them in a suite next to my father's. I spent little time with

Dad. He gave me a five-dollar-a-day allowance and bought me dinner. I had to be there right at dinnertime or did without.

I saw my mother as much as possible and had fun visiting with her and cheering her up. In the meantime, Dad was parading his different girl friends up to his suite every night.

I was starting to notice girls and *really* noticed The Book Ends. But I was a slow starter. I didn't really start dating until I got into college.

In any event, I was sitting in the audience one night listening to Dad's band at the Royal Hawaiian. Candy, one of The Book Ends, had her mother over and I was sitting with her at a table when Dad invited me to come up onstage and play a trumpet solo with the band. I was reticent because I'd never played with a famous band or in a big hotel before. It is one thing to solo at school and another to get up and play in a professional situation. Candy's mother urged me—"Perry, go on up." I was scared, but I went.

Dad handed me the trumpet and said, "Be careful with the mouthpiece. I don't know what kind of girls you've been kissing." The audience laughed—funny line. I beamed. My father was joking with his son. So I got to play at the Royal Hawaiian. I played "The Sound of Music"—it was my best number. I received a standing ovation and was pleased that my father could be proud of me. Then he played his big hit, "Young Man with the Horn." Some drunk yelled from the audience, "Bring the kid back!" That did not go over very well with Dad. He did *not* bring the kid back.

Another time I visited him at work in Las Vegas all I did was play screamers like Maynard Ferguson, my father's idol. He couldn't very well not invite me up if I was in the audience because anybody and everybody in the business was getting to know that I played trumpet. But I was upstaging *him*—the young man with the horn—second generation. He didn't want to be the older generation.

I was a good student in high school. A Christian school is close—like a family. It might have been macho to play football, but I was in the band, getting better and better at trumpet. Music was a release for me and a subliminal way of getting closer to my father. I didn't realize until a year or so ago the effect the trumpet had on me. I gave it up for a year because it made me think of my father—and of his disowning me.

Dad never liked me being in a Christian school and told me so. He thought I was being perverted. Mom never had me baptized because Dad was Catholic and she was Lutheran. I was baptized in my mother's faith when I was old enough to know what I wanted. Dad was also opposed to my attending a school that did not believe in premarital sex. He just couldn't handle the fact that I might grow up with a different set of morals than his.

Seems like I was forever changing schools. In tenth grade, I went through another of those difficult transitions. My grandparents moved to Yucca Valley out in the desert—really the rural community to end all rural communities. Once again I was different, so right away it was assumed that I was gay. I was treated like the campus queer. Somebody was always on my back. I'd never fought anybody because I'd been taught that fighting was wrong. I had been protected. Now I was on my own without all that protection. I hid and even avoided some of my own friends. It was the hardest time of my life—knowing that I was not liked by my schoolmates.

My sexual identity was traumatic. I was being accused of something that was not in my nature. I like girls too much to have a sexual relationship with a guy. That's when my faith in God really saw me through a time when I was totally unable to cope on my own.

In my junior year, I was close to a nervous breakdown. I talked it over with Grandma and she understood. I moved back with Mom, who was living at Newport. She gave up her one-bedroom apartment and took a larger, more expensive place so I could be with her. The world was bright again.

Almost instantaneously, I became a different person. My suicidal thoughts departed—I only wanted to live and enjoy life. Still, I faced the uncertainties of entering a new school—again. I wanted to be liked but feared the same experiences I'd had in the past. What a surprise I was in for! At Estonsia, my new school, which had just won the band sweepstakes trophy for band revue, I was welcomed into the band.

A party atmosphere permeates the beach community in Southern California, and now that I lived there, I partied more, too. I was in a school that accepted me for myself and liked me. Being part of the activities that went on, I felt important to my school, my class—and to myself. I developed a crush on a girl. She was cute but I was clumsy. I was just winging it, but having a good time, anyway.

During my senior year, my father came down to hear me play in concert with the stage band. I thought he was making an attempt to be a father. I wanted to believe that. He was building a new house and asked me to work for him that summer, which I did.

I graduated at midterm and was enrolled in Orange Coast College where I started playing tennis because Dad was a great tennis buff. I was a natural. I played five hours a day. My trumpet playing improved because of lessons I was taking from Harold Mitchell who was Ollie Mitchell's father. He was a great teacher and it was my first *formal* education with the horn. At seventy-one he had it all together musically. I, too, seemed to be getting it together. I was a very busy young man.

I even entertained ideas of perhaps going to live with my father. I thought we were getting closer, now that we were playing tennis almost every day. Sometimes I even doubled with some of his friends. Tennis became my driving force. Tennis and trumpet. I dropped all my classes except band at Orange Coast.

Being in college was a real change of pace for me. All the pettiness of elementary and secondary schools was gone. My graduation from high school was no big thing. Mom was out of town and Dad didn't attend. I passed up grad night even though I'd paid for it. I didn't have a date, so I stayed home.

During that summer Dad had me working on his new house—strictly menial stuff at minimum wage, but hell, I figured it was for my dad. I kept saying to myself, "I'm his only heir, so why not." I should have known better. I was used. Just another Ray Anthony "possession."

Also, my grandmother lived with him—and still does. She never liked my mother or me. I think she saw Mom as a threat to her own position in Dad's life.

It was a trying summer. I played tennis with Dad and his friends. In doubles I began beating my father. Once again it was more than he could handle—being beaten by the younger generation. Every kid wants to beat his father at things—just to show he's equal.

Mom taught me who was and who wasn't a good friend and I was discovering that I had some friends now. I also had money, but was always overdrawn at the bank. Mom was very liberal with money. Dad paid a minimal amount of child support and that was it. No extras unless it was a bribe to keep my mother from enforcing the child support order.

Orange Coast was OK, but I wanted to attend a religious school. Dad told me to forget it. "You don't need to go to college," he said. "I'll get you a job. Maybe you can start as a pool sweeper—learn a trade." It was as if he didn't want me to succeed. I had always been told that my father would pay for my college education for a B.A. degree or for six years following high school. I took it for granted that's the way it would be, assuming he had set aside the twenty-five thousand dollars required. He'd certainly never told me any differently.

He objected adamantly to a private *Christian* college. We had a terrible fight over that. The issue was finally settled in a courtroom.

My beliefs are quite different from those of my parents. I believe that premarital sex is wrong. They don't. Mom accepted my personal morals code. Dad tried to dissuade me. On my twenty-first birthday he took me to a massage parlor. I suppose that was his idea of introducing me to manhood. It is difficult to understand what he thought.

In spite of my father's objections, I ·attended the school of my choice. In the court hearings Dad's lawyers shocked everybody by calling me a fraud, a cheat, and a carouser. My father sat there without batting an eyelash.

One thing was interesting. He knew that eventually he would have to pay, so he started looking for schools with a cheaper tuition. I suggested USC as an alternative— it was the most expensive. Dad couldn't see that at all, but I could see where his heart was—in his wallet.

The last day in court the judge looked at Dad from the bench and asked, "Aren't you Ray Anthony the entertainer?"

"Yes," he answered.

"Well, I can't understand why you wouldn't want your son to better himself. You are deducting thousands of dollars a year off your income tax as car expense—and your son's tuition is only about forty-five hundred dollars a year." That was a drop in the bucket to what he had spent on his new house. The judge ordered my tuition to be paid by Dad and that ended that. Or so I thought. He got behind in the tuition payments and because I plan to go on to law school and don't want to leave owing the school money, I called him about it. He said, "You know, I've disinherited you. You're not getting one dime out of me."

"I know," I said. "Why do you think I'm so anxious to get an education? I want to support myself." He hung up on me. The court has decided that Mom and Dad will divide my tuition for law school.

Although it is difficult to think of my life as being any different than it has been, I would have been much happier with just plain ordinary everyday working parents who were at home in a family setting. I'm certain of one thing. When I marry it will be for life and my family will be the most important thing in the world to me.

Margaret's father, Richard Whiting

Margaret Whiting today
Courtesy of Margaret Whiting

Margaret Whiting with members of the cast from the Allied Artists film *Paris Follies of 1956*, in which she starred.

Courtesy of Larry Edmunds

11

Margaret Whiting

The daughter of songwriter Richard Whiting, Margaret went on to her own superstardom as a singer of songs and recording artist at Capitol Records where she recorded hit after hit throughout the forties and into the fifties. She is one of very few children of celebrities whose success equaled that of her famous parent.

As a youngster, her father was the parent for whom she really cared. Their relationship was perfect in Margaret's eyes and it was only after she was grown and into therapy that she was able to reconcile the resentment and rebellion she felt toward her mother.

She is an emotional lady who tries to conceal that emotion with an exterior that "can handle any situation." I suspect she cries easily, is vulnerable, and filled with love and compassion for whomever she comes into contact. Hers was a professional life from her earliest days at the studio with her father, where she inspired him to write "On the Good Ship Lollipop" for another little girl—

Shirley Temple. Her family was not nouveau riche and she seems to have avoided the affectation or snobbishness so typical of children whose parents were overnight "discoveries." Margaret Whiting is a *real* lady.

I'll never forget a remark Ava Gardner made to me. We were at our attorney's house one evening and she was sitting at my feet by the coffee table. I said, "My God, I've never seen anybody who looked so beautiful without makeup. You are really one of the beautiful women of the screen. No, forget the screen—beautiful in every way—but beautiful."

She responded, "I only wanted my husbands to feel that. To love me for me. [Mickey Rooney and Artie Shaw—Frank Sinatra came later.] I tried so hard to make Artie love me and not the star. I also tried to be his equal intellectually. I just wanted someone to love me for me."

That's always stuck with me. This beautiful, vulnerable woman looking up at me and saying, "I wanted to be loved for me." When you are in show business, you are loved for the buck you can make and if you're the child of an entertainment celebrity, that knowledge is an early part of your education. I'm a very happy woman today largely because I've never reached the emotional heights or the depths that so many people I know who came out of the business have.

My roots were once in Hollywood. I say that in the past tense deliberately. I've recently had a resurgence in my singing career thanks to Four Girls Four, a traveling quartet composed of big band singers including Rosemary Clooney, Helen O'Connell, and myself—all big band veterans—and Rose Marie. The group has been very popular and once again I find myself out on the road entertaining. On the tours, I carry books because I love to read and I carry certain things that are very much part of my house.

I'm jumping all over the place, but I've lived in big homes in Hollywood most of my life. About fourteen years ago I picked up my roots and transplanted them to New York because that's what *I* wanted to do. I realized the day I put my key in the door to my Manhattan apartment that the roots are me, not the house. Today my roots are in Room 1200 of the Ramada Inn in Beverly Hills. Tomorrow I'll probably be in Detroit or Chicago and that will become my roots.

Thanks to my upbringing in a celebrity atmosphere, I learned that the show must go on and you are responsible for yourself when you're in the spotlight. I've gotten to know myself and my saying is this: I stand on my own feet and say "you got yourself into this, so you better have enough guts to get yourself out of it, kid, when the going goes bad."

I'm into Science of Mind, which is an adjunct to any religion—just positive thinking with no doors closed. Mary Baker Eddy, the founder of Science of Mind, didn't believe in doctors. I do. I stand for positive thinking. Raised a Catholic, I get up every morning and thank God for living and what he's brought me. I care for people. I'm so appreciative of everything I was given and inherited. From my mother I've inherited a wonderful sense of humor; from my father, my singing talent. I resented my mother for such a long time and it was only years after I became an adult that I fully realized how terrific she was. People say to me, "You're such a survivor." Well, I inherit that from Eleanor, my mother. I resented her because I didn't understand her. Actually, I'm *earthy*. Example: When I was in Seattle with the girls, Rosemary and I hung out together and we shopped and went to the mountains and just looked at the beautiful scenery. Great fun. First day I get into town I love to walk and see where the good restaurants are. I don't have to have a lot of hangers-on or an entourage. Most of that comes from my mother and for years I didn't know it. Mother was different and I'm different and my daughter now realizes that she is also different.

My daughter Debby is terrific. We went through some bad times together, but we survived. I'm different as a mother in that I just don't fit into the category of being a *mother* mother. My mother didn't either. But she gave me tenacity. My father had great musicianship and gentility and a sense of humor, too. Once he said, "Margaret, there's all kinds of music in the world and I love it all, but some people don't. Never be afraid to expose yourself to all music. At least you'll learn there is a whole spectrum of music as there is of life. You don't have to accept it all, you don't have to like it all, but at least know that it is there."

In retrospect I know you also don't *have* to love your mother necessarily.

The greatest memories of childhood for me are of my father. Especially when I was allowed to sit with him at the piano when he'd come home from the studio in the evenings. He would play his new songs or he'd get Richard Rodgers and Lorenz Hart's new songs or Kern's and he'd teach me all this wonderful music and say, "Here's Jerry Kern's new hit." I started singing with him when I was very very young. He would say, "No, that's not the way to do it. We take a long time writing these songs. Sing it simply. Sing it honestly. Sing the notes the way we write them and make the songs important." That was always the greatest kick for me.

I was a loner. I have a sister, Barbara, five years younger than I. I was born in Detroit and was three years old when we moved to Hollywood, so my earliest memories are actually from the West Coast. Our home was in the Hollywood Hills, and although I don't remember this, when Mother and Dad wanted to go out for the evening,

Oscar Levant would be my baby-sitter. An eccentric and recognized authority on Gershwin music, Levant baby-sat because he was crazy about my father's Steinway and would spend the evening with his finger adulating the piano keys while I sat wide-eyed listening to the beautiful music he produced on my father's piano. We later moved into a large house on Ambassador Drive just below the Jack Warner estate.

My father adored playing golf and let me walk around the golf courses with him almost every day when he got home from work. I loved those times. They were like a great outdoors adventure for me. He usually played with other songwriters—Johnny Mercer, Harold Arlen, Jerome Kern, and Harry Warren—all great men.

In school, I was very shy. Until he died, my whole life was wrapped around my father. He was the greatest of all influences in my life. Mother managed our wonderful house and took care of all the accounting for my father as well as planning and giving parties for Dad. She arranged everything so he could be alone and wouldn't have two kids making noise while he worked at home.

I was crazy about magazines and still am. But as a young girl I was absolutely obsessed with them. I'd go around the house collecting all the magazines and take them up to my room where I'd hide them in drawers until I'd collected seven or eight issues and then start reading them. I was very protective and didn't want anyone to know where they were. To this day, I have no idea why. When I am out on the road singing it is not unusual for me to be toting forty pounds of magazines around.

My life was pleasant and I went to school and watched this very strong woman, my mother, manipulating our lives (I rebelled against that constantly), molding us all—manipulating my father, caring for him with great love and affection. I never remember a harsh word be-

Margaret Whiting ☆ 181

tween them. Only the beautiful music with which I grew up. Knowing how devoted I was to my father, my mother wisely sat me down and had a long talk with me when my sister Barbara was born.

"You know," she said, "your father wanted a boy and we got you and we love you very much, so I really shouldn't have another child, but I wanted to try to give your father a son. So we have another daughter and she's here and we're going to love her." Mother was very perceptive and I never resented the new baby. I was really my father's girl and what was important to me was that he loved me. I'd often accompany him to the studio and he'd play all the songs for me. I remember one day he was having a terrible time trying to write a song for a kid doing a picture at 20th Century Fox.

He turned to me and asked, "I've got to do something young—about a young girl, a kid. What can I do? It must be something that typifies the scene." I was eating candy— a big lollipop—and dripping the sticky stuff all over the place. Daddy said, "Take that lollipop away. You're getting it all over the piano." Then he sat down and wrote "On the Good Ship Lollipop." The picture was *Bright Eyes.* The kid at Fox was Shirley Temple. Daddy always told me I was responsible for that song and every time I hear it I laugh. There I was, dripping goo all over his piano and he was inspired to write an all-time favorite song for a little girl who became an institution. It's a great story and I love it.

Eleven years isn't much. That's how old I was when my father died. Eleven. But the thing is, I could sing. They tell me when I was two in Detroit my father would play a record of one of his songs and I would hear one note and immediately could tell what the song would be. So it was obvious that I was going to sing. My Aunt Margaret Young had been a big singing star in vaudeville and introduced "Way Down Yonder in New Orleans" and "Oh, Johnny, Oh!" Mother had been her agent and manager.

They were a family of thirteen. Mother was the youngest, but she saw the talent Aunt Margaret had and kept pushing her. Incidentally, I was named after her. Anyway, off they went on the road. Mother's best friend was Sophie Tucker and she managed her for a little while, too. Daddy was a song plugger for Jerome Remmick in Detroit. Born in Peoria, Illinois, he moved on to Detroit, a thriving city in those days, a hub of activity with the young auto industry coming into its own as a mover of a soon-to-be-traveling America. He played the new songs being published by Mr. Remmick or whatever else was popular. He would play the new songs for Margaret and Eleanor, my mother, would judge them alone.

Daddy was taking Aunt Margaret out and then one day, he switched to Mother and ended up marrying her. In 1929 or 1930 Mother decided that Daddy had to make a decision about his future. One day she cornered him and said, "The time has come. You either will go to New York and write shows or you will go to Hollywood where it is beginning to happen. [Talkies were new and revolutionizing the film industry.] You just cannot continue living in Detroit. It is not right for your career." Of course, as it turned out she was absolutely right. It was the time of the Wall Street crash and eve of the Great Depression of the thirties.

He then wrote "Ain't We Got Fun," a song typical of the depression. Fortunately we were not to fall victim to the times. Mother and Dad packed up and we moved out to California where he was signed as a songwriter by Paramount Pictures. Then he went to 20th Century Fox and I think he did a couple of pictures at MGM. During his last years he collaborated with the great Johnny Mercer, an unhappy man who produced such wonderful lyrics.

Happy lyrics. At the time Mercer had been working with Bing Crosby and was with the Paul Whiteman Band. Buddy Morris, head of Wittmark and Warners Music, signed Mercer. Morris was the professional manager and he said, "Mercer is coming out to write this picture and he'll either write with Whiting or Borek." Of course, he eventually wrote with both.

My father was a traditionalist. Loved holidays—especially the Fourth of July because of the fireworks. The Fourth of July was the biggie for us. Dad would start with fireworks bright and early in the morning and we'd be shooting them off into the night. There was always a big picnic in our garden with loads of friends joining us for the festivities. It was a Hollywood much different from what is there today. Dad was a terrific golfer and had he not been such a great songwriter he might have entered the professional golf circuit and done quite well. He always shot in the low sixties. In any event, to make a point, he had all sorts of cups he'd won at amateur and pro/am tournaments. When he died and we were going through the painful task of sorting out his personal possessions we found that every single one of those golf cups was jammed full of firecrackers. I have to smile thinking about that because he and his golfing pals were always playing practical jokes on one another. I remember that whenever he played with Kern or Warren or Gus Kahn, just as they'd tee off Dad would drop a firecracker and it would just drive them crazy. But they always managed to get even with their own pranks.

Birthdays were also special, as was Christmas, which was the best. Big trees, big parties—always parties. As I grew up, those fabulous "Saturday nights at the Whitings" with all the great singers and songwriters were a Hollywood tradition, if anything in Hollywood can be considered traditional.

Mother was a great party giver and on Saturday nights the place abounded with the people Dad loved—Maurice Chevalier, Leo McCarey, and Buddy De Sylva, Daddy's best friend. Big producers like Ernst Lubitsch came. I wasn't allowed to attend those adult parties, but I'd look down from our house on Beverly Glen with its big Spanish balcony and red curtains. Look down and hear all those people playing the piano and singing. It drove me nuts because I couldn't be with them. Johnny Mercer used to tell me, "I'd look up and there would be little Margaret peeking through."

Once, when I was six or seven, I came downstairs and was allowed to sing a couple of songs for Mercer. He applauded me and said, "You've got it. You're going to do it." He turned to my father and said, "Richard, she's going to be wonderful. She's got to find a style and practice and everything, but she's going to be a singer." What encouragement from someone I so greatly admired!

My father worked with me a great deal and taught me all of the necessities for my future craft. I think I always knew I would sing. Daddy would take me over to Harry Warren's house on Coldwater Canyon for weekends and he would play for me. I liked to hang around with "Uncle" Harry. Mrs. Gus Kahn once said to my mother, "Don't worry about Vassar or any of those schools. Show biz, that's it. No matter what you do, forget all the rest. She'll be in show biz and that's it—so relax."

My father wanted both Barbara and me to have a good education. He said, "It is so important because it will give you something to fall back on." Daddy was both gifted and moneyed. Money had been in his family for generations. I can still hear him: "Margaret, education is so important."

On the other hand, my mother felt it was important to be your own person and to be able to "do your own thing," and stand on your own two feet. She didn't like dependency on other people. One must be able to handle any situation, to be self-reliant. There were very few traumatic situations with my father but many later on with Mother. Oh, my God, how I resented her and rebelled against her at one point in my life—all because I was young and headstrong and didn't comprehend the thrust of her intentions for me. Of course, all of that changed when I matured enough to see the validity of her particular type of encouragement.

Most of my friends were from within the entertainment industry. Harry Warren's daughter Cookie, Irene and David Kahn, Otto Klemperer's daughter Lottie, Anna and Jerry Bowmont, Betsy Bloomingdale, Carol Houston —mostly the daughters and sons of my father's friends. Cookie was my very close friend.

I was very secretive; as outgoing as I am now, as a girl I was just the opposite and led a very private life. I can't think of anything I did that would have shocked my family, but I'm sure Mother would remember such incidents better than I. She used to write notes to me. She never talked to me very much. It was her habit to slip notes under my door. "Do this." "Do that." "Don't go out with this boy." "Don't go out with that boy." Notes that aggravated me something awful at the time.

The most traumatic thing that ever happened to me was the death of my father. I would eventually have to deal with that in therapy. My mother didn't really want me to see him die because she knew how much I loved him. I felt unfairly left out. I wanted to be with him. He had a heart attack from high blood pressure. Dad was a very nervous man. Recently I went to see a Gershwin show and it was interesting because my father and George Gershwin were very close friends. George brought my father to New York to see *Porgy and Bess*. Gershwin died in

July of 1937 and Dad attended his funeral. Although it had nothing to do with Gershwin, really, my father died in November of that same year. He was a nervous man, as I say, and he began to fail rather suddenly.

I wanted three things from my father: a trip to Hawaii, a silver fox coat, and a swimming pool. He said, "You are much too young for the silver fox coat. Eleanor and I will take care of that later. The trip to Hawaii, we'll see about. And the pool? Well, we'll see about that, too." One day in the spring of 1937 I came home from school and the men were in the garden digging a big hole for our new swimming pool—my pool. It was April when the pool was christened. It had been too cold to go in, but I christened it anyway. I spent that last wonderful summer with him. That's when George Gershwin died. At the end of summer he began to fail.

Nevertheless, we spent every day during the summer in that pool and had a wonderful time, until I saw him start to disintegrate. He was finally hospitalized for a while and then brought home. He didn't want me to see him in his robe getting smaller and smaller, so Mother talked it over with Leo Robbin, who was a very close friend to our family, and I moved to his house for a month. Dad came home from the hospital in September and I guess by then Mother knew there wasn't a chance. Dad would tell her, when she related that I wanted to see him, "I don't want Margaret to see me like this." I came over every day anyway just to be near him. Then, on the morning of November 12, Leo Robbins woke me up—it was Saturday morning. He said, "I've got bad news for you."

I said, "I know. Daddy died." He took me home and it is the only time I can ever remember my mother putting her arms around me. She said, "Well now, there are just three of us. We'll take care of one another." I wasn't allowed to go to the funeral and I don't know if that was good or bad. My therapist told me, "I don't know either, Margaret, but Eleanor was really trying to protect you and that wonderful image you had of your father. That wonderful love. She didn't want you to see anything like that."

I probably held that against her for years. That all came out in therapy. I hadn't been allowed to share the grief and I resented being left out of it.

I'll tell you something interesting, and I'm just now putting this together. My ex-husband, Lou Busch, died not too long ago and it was something I could share with my daughter—the feeling of losing a father one loved so dearly. Speaking of her father's funeral, she said, "You know, Mom, my dad was wonderful."

I said, "I know. You're telling me."

She continued, "I went up to the house and then to the funeral home to look at the body and dress him. I had to be strong." Lou had done the Joe Fingers Carr Barroom piano thing and she said she had thought it was something he'd like to be remembered for. "I was just dying to throw some garters into the casket in remembrance of that, but out of deference to his wife [he was remarried] I didn't. He would have loved it."

Lou was killed in an automobile accident—went over a cliff—and had a lot of bruises on his face. Debby said, "That wasn't my daddy. He looked beautiful, but it wasn't Daddy." But you know what was so wonderful for me? She had the opportunity to hear her father eulogized. The King Sisters sang and Steve Allen did the narration. "It was wonderful, Mother. Afterward we went over to the King Sisters' house and they had a big party for us. It was a happy and marvelous moment. They even had a kinescope of Daddy and Lincoln Moraga playing for a concert. That was so terrific. I was crying. I never knew his first wife, Janet Blair, but we had our arms around each other and we shared the moment."

So my daughter has a memory—will always have the memory. I never had that—something else I blamed on my mother.

Following my father's passing, life changed rapidly for me. Career took over almost immediately. I was going to school; I think I was the only girl who ever went to Marymount who became a professional singer. They wouldn't let me sing, but they let me act. So I played the lead in a lot of the plays.

My aunt Margaret came out to California because my mother was very lonely and they had always been so close. Peter Lind Hayes's mother had a place out in the valley called Grace Hayes's Lodge. It was located right at Coldwater Canyon and Ventura Boulevard. All the stars used to go out to Grace's. Peter was just beginning his career. My aunt took me out one night and I got up and sang. Then I sang again another night when both my mother and aunt were there. I loved it. This was a couple of years after Daddy died.

So I would go out, get up and sing, and have fun—but more importantly, I was being noticed. We had some arrangements made and Grace put me to work for a couple of weeks in her club—at one hundred dollars a week. It was done under the table, because I was way under age to be performing for money in a club.

Meanwhile I was going to school. One day I had a chance to go on an NBC radio program with Johnny Mercer. Johnny was a guest and Bobby Sherwood and Skitch Henderson were two of the musicians. Skitch had been around our house and lived with us for two years because he was accompanying my aunt Margaret—she planned to sing again. The first day he came to rehearsal with her she said, "This is my niece and she sings well."

Skitch said, "Let me hear her sing." He played "Give Me the Simple Life," and I've never stopped singing from that day. I worked with Skitch every day and I learned songs. Skitch asked Johnny Mercer to bring me down to the radio show. The show was called *One Half Hour.* Skitch was like a big brother to me. It was a local show out of Hollywood airing in the morning. I sang one of my father's songs—"My Ideal"—on that first show. I had a hit record of that song in the forties and continue to include it in my repertoire. The NBC people heard me and signed me to a contract for a couple of years—singing on what were known as "sustaining programs," which meant fitting me in wherever a singer was needed, and believe me, I got lots of exposure. Charles Dent and Gordon Jenkins were the conductors, so I had the opportunity to sing with a big orchestra. They made all the arrangements and I'd sing maybe five or six times a week and loved every minute of it. How wonderful, working with such professional greats.

One day Johnny Mercer came to me and said, "Margaret, I'm going to start a record company. Would you like to record?" Would I? Indeed! So I was the first artist he signed at Capitol Records. I was in at the beginning of what has become a recording empire.

The first record I made at Capitol was with the Les Brown Band, fronted by Billy Butterfield with arrangements by Paul Weston. Capitol was actually owned by Glen Wallich who owned Music City (a big record store at Sunset and Vine), Buddy De Sylva and Johnny Mercer.

Johnny said, "Margaret, I'd like you to sing a song of mine on your first recording. I want you to do 'My Ideal' and 'Without Love.'" That was to be the first record, but Johnny had written a song called "Old Black Magic." He wanted Freddie Slack's orchestra to record it, but Freddie's singer, Ella Mae Morse, couldn't sing it, so they came to me. That became the very first record that came from Capitol and it did very well. "My Ideal" followed and the next thing that happened was "Moonlight in Vermont," which became a smash hit for me. World War II was on. I was still a teen-ager and somehow servicemen and civilians all over the world associated with that song. You want to know something? I've never been in Vermont. An interesting aspect to that song is that the original lyrics had the word *tow* in them. I asked Johnny, "What is a tow?" He said, "No problem. We'll change it to 'Ski Trails.'" With *ski tow* replaced by *ski trails,* the song became a hit and a standard.

To show you just how luck or happenstance comes into play—even with great music—let me explain how another of my hits came about. In 1945, Capitol said they would let me do a record of my choice with Paul Weston. I decided on a Mercer/Warren tune from the film *The Harvey Girls* called "My Intuition," which Judy Garland was singing in the picture. It was to be backed by "Blue Skies" because Bing Crosby was reviving that. A great record. Everybody in Hollywood came to the recording session. Forty-piece band—terrific. The week before the record was to come out, Arthur Freed, the film's producer, threw the song out of the picture and we were stuck with a side of the record to do.

I'd been over at 20th Century Fox baby-sitting my sister while she starred in *Junior Miss.* I'd heard about a song from Rodgers and Hart's *State Fair,* which was being shot there with Dick Haymes and Jeanne Crain. Director George Seaton played the entire score for me and one song, "It Might as Well Be Spring," appealed to me. I told Paul Weston about it and he came over. Barbara Ford, John Ford's daughter, was the assistant cutter on the picture and she played it for us again. Paul listened and then said, "That's great." Overnight he made the arrangement and we recorded it the next day, rushed it out, and it was number one on the charts for nine months. That really solidified my career and future as a singer.

I was a teen-ager and as a teen-ager I rebelled against my mother. Did everything she said not to do. Don't go out with this fellow. I went. Go to bed early. I stayed up late. I'd go out with the wrong people to all the wrong places in defiance. I dated a lot of musicians, which may or may not have been the right thing to do, but I thought it was terrific. My mother, of course, didn't agree. That was my form of rebellion.

I'm a very disciplined person and I don't think I've really, strangely enough, done anything in my life that was detrimental to me. I cannot imagine putting drugs into my body. I smoked one joint in my life and slept for twelve hours. It was sensational. I could never see taking pills or have to face life with liquor. I understand it, but it doesn't work for me. So I was never destructive to myself as I grew up. The only destructive things I may have done involved my relationships with men. Always picking the wrong one (probably to be sure it wasn't going to work, I guess). I never played the game in Hollywood. Never attended the parties or dated the "right" people. I didn't feel I had to. I didn't want to. I mean, as a teen-ager, I did what I wanted to do without worrying about it. I was now rebelling against the establishment instead of my mother.

Even my first sexual experience. It was no accident. I planned it. I wasn't in love. I wanted to get it over with because my mother had painted such a dour picture of sex. I got myself in a position where I was sure it would happen and then I *did* have something to drink. Just to say to hell with it, to have the courage to get it over with. Believe me, it wasn't like my mother told me—it wasn't like anything anybody had told me. It was just one drink, a hell of a nice guy—an experience. Afterward, I didn't walk around and yell, "Hey, I'm no longer a virgin." I just wanted to find out what it was all about. My mother was the kind of woman who said, "Sex is one thing and love is the most important thing. Guys will just have sex with you and they won't give a damn about you." What a bad picture to present to a young teen-age girl! I was practical in my approach to the whole thing. I wanted to know *exactly* what it was all about. Later on it became a joy because I loved the man. I thank God that first experience was not a bad situation that would have turned me off.

Actually it was comparable to the way I approach life. I take a song, for instance, and get the foundation of it. Then I begin to break it up and find out what it is all about. Sort of make three acts out of a song, a ballad. What is "Send in the Clowns"? What is that really about? What does it mean? How can I give a different meaning? How can I make it work as the actress? Learn it first and then put in the nuances. Not too different from sex.

Barbara and I were never competitors. She was the actress and I more the singer. When we did our television show together I said, "Let's change our last names. Let's think of ourselves as two actresses. Let's not let the emotion of being sisters, even though it is working, get in our way. We mustn't do The Andrews Sisters. That would be a disaster for us." So we were always very much our own people—individuals who happened to be sisters.

Eleanor was more a problem for me than Barbara. My mother was really Rose, in a way, from *Gypsy*. I think Mother must have wanted to be a singer and couldn't make it. She used to tell me stories about Max Gordon (the producer) and Irving Berlin—and others—wanting her to go on, but she'd get up there and couldn't do it. So I think she probably saw in me some of the things she wanted to do and couldn't and really pushed me.

She would talk to Buddy De Sylva and he'd say, "Oh, for Christ's sake, Eleanor, leave Margaret alone. I tried to stay away from all that nonsense, found my own agent, and was signed to do *Your Hit Parade*. I didn't sing with a

Margaret Whiting ☆ 193

beat so George Washington Hill fired me for singing behind the beat. I was more into phrasing.

I am always asked my opinion of Christina Crawford's book. Frankly, I don't know her attitude. I know
how people who adored Crawford feel. Hell, all the people who claim to be great parents aren't necessarily black,
white, or pink—they're a lot of grays, you know. I think it
was great therapy for Christina.

Regrets about being brought up in "the Hollywood
tradition"? Not many. Now that I travel a lot I wish I'd not
ignored history and geography—the world—when I was a
student. It infuriates me that I fluffed off those courses.
Anyway, I was a lousy student. I liked to sing and hang
out with the guys and that was it. While a lot of girls were
doing homework in the evenings, I was down at Capitol
Records grinding out hit tunes.

I wish my father could have lived longer. Not only for
Barbara and me, but so the world could have enjoyed
more of his great talent. He would have coped with today's music and not been as bitter as some songwriters are.
I would like to see what he would have written. I wish I'd
been able to understand my mother more as I was growing
up because I now understand her motives. I'd like to know
why she taught me so well but never really communicated
with me. I'm sure she thought she did, but she didn't.
There was a lot of unnecessary loneliness, for instance the
notes she left under my door instead of a warm conversation.

I grew up in a period of normal madness. That was
Hollywood in the late thirties and early forties. The war
was on. I am a child of that electrifying period and I don't
resent it.

William Katt as he appears today in his hit television series, *The Greatest American Hero*.

William (Billy) Katt on the left, sister Jody, father Bill Williams, pet collie, mother Barbara Hale, and younger sister Juanita in yard of their San Fernando Valley home when Billy was a youngster.

Courtesy of Barbara Hale

12

William Katt

For a Hollywood kid who certainly went through his share of mischief and mayhem, Barbara Hale and Bill Williams's son Billy has made it through the obstacle courses that are unique to the offspring of celebrities. After battles with drugs and envy of noncelebrity offspring, he has emerged reasonably unscathed.

Barbara Hale, better known today as The Amana Lady, was a household word as Della Street, the faithful and loyal secretary to Perry Mason. Along with Billy Katt's father, Bill Williams, she starred in feature films where they met, fell in love, married, and theoretically rode off into the sunset happily ever after. Billy is one of three children of Barbara and Bill Williams. The happy trails were often strewn with tumbleweed and cactus. Billy only hinted at the frictions between his parents, the stress brought on by the competitive nature of acting and two careers in the same family. When Bill was starring as Kit

Carson and Barbara was on *Perry Mason,* all was well. When one was out of work, the hassles would begin.

Their son is now a star of his own TV show *(The Greatest American Hero)* and seems to be following in his parents' footsteps. His career seems assured and his stardom may surpass that of his parents, but he has learned the harsh lessons of stardom firsthand and doesn't want his wife to compete with him—and she doesn't.

Much of my early childhood was spent—or so it seems—sitting between the legs of a horse watching my father film his television series, *Kit Carson.*

An experience that left a very strong impression with me involved traveling with Dad to do charity appearances for spastic children. He took me with him to Albuquerque on the train, which was in and of itself a big excitement for me. There we were, father and son; he in his Kit Carson outfit and me with a junior version of the same. I was about five or six and obviously had no reservations about being out on stage in front of several thousand children. I've since learned that a little kid can do pretty much as he wants on stage and get away with it. It was my first taste of appearing before an audience and in retrospect I suppose one could say I enjoyed the experience.

Both my parents have influenced my life. There's a bond between my father and me that has grown from a child/parent relationship to what is now a very strong man-to-man tie. We respect each other. I can't say that we have always enjoyed a perfect relationship, because that's just not true. There's always been a good feeling with my mother (even when we were at odds), but there was a time when things were somewhat rough between my dad and me. I don't know if it was any different from any other father/son experience, but I went through a rebellious stage when I first became a teen-ager.

My rebellion stemmed from what I considered generation contradictions. My parents would tell me not to do certain things that they did. I wanted my independence at an early age and they just didn't see it my way—especially my father. I resented on the one hand hearing that "you're now becoming an adult," and on the other hand not being adult enough to be independent. So one goes out and gets into mischief. I did.

Growing up in the San Fernando Valley of Los Angeles in the late fifties and early sixties was very boring. There simply wasn't much for a teen-ager to do. No real activities. No clubs. Consequently many of us got to be what old-timers used to call "hellions." We certainly didn't have the gang activity that was already popping up in Venice and some parts of East Los Angeles. Only recently have gangs become noticeable in the San Fernando Valley. We were just young people trying to find some excitement.

Sometimes we hung out at drive-ins eating hamburgers and french fries while listening to The Stones on the jukeboxes. Other times we did stupid things like joyriding in someone's car without permission. A better and more honest description would be "riding around in stolen automobiles." I was very fortunate not to have gotten myself into some real trouble. Fortunate in the sense that I never got caught.

The San Fernando Valley was and is suburbia. At that time it was considered somewhat rural suburbia by the more sophisticated Beverly Hills celebrity village. A number of film and television personalities lived in the valley—and still do. Often they bought property as an investment and sold off parcels, leaving enough room for their own homes with spacious landscaping. Nobody ever said they were going to visit Sherman Oaks (where I grew up). It was always, "going over to the valley." It was almost the middle-America type of community that commentators and politicians like to speak of—only with a larger population.

I spent ninth grade at the Army Navy Academy in Carlsbad, California. Later I would go on to Grant High School in Van Nuys where I eventually graduated. Most boys are dragged by the hair of the head to military schools, but I volunteered for the academy. I was at that belligerent stage of my life when I hated my father and my mother. It was a case of wanting to get away from home—get from under the yoke of parental authority. Love had nothing to do with it. I always loved my parents and knew they felt the same about me. Still, things had become so tense in my life I had to make a decision. That decision was to go to military school—because it was away from home. I had friends enrolled at the prestigious Harvard Military Academy near my home. Unfortunately my grades weren't good enough for me to get in there, so I opted for the Army Navy Academy—to escape authority. Boy was I dumb!

It was my first lengthy period away from home and my first introduction to some real characters. It didn't take long for some students to find out that I came from a celebrity family. A few will take advantage of such circumstances, often cruelly. One kid did. It was pure extortion. He would beat me up every Friday if I didn't cough up a couple of bucks for his weekend—all because he knew who my parents were. I endured that.

At the academy I was introduced to drugs for the first time. Once I got my feet wet, I think I tried most of the drugs going around at the time, but not any of the hard stuff. I don't like drugs—not as a habit. I don't like the feeling of being out of control of myself. As an adult I prefer an occasional beer. But how do you tell a teen-ager

it is stupid to use drugs when he has manhood at his fin-
gertips—but not quite?

A very bad experience with a psychedelic drug
changed my life and since then I've never done anything
psychedelic. It was during the height of the Beatles craze
in the mid-sixties. I was sixteen. One day while driving
over Laurel Canyon, one of those roads that twists and
turns like a traveling snake between the mountains that
separate Hollywood and the valley, I picked up some
long-haired kids. One of them offered me some acid. It
looked like gumdrops. I said, "Sure. Fine. Why not?" No
big deal. Several hours later at a girl friend's house the full
effect hit me. (I would later learn it was really bad acid—
probably laced with strychnine.) I coped—or tried to
cope—for several days. I needed help and knew it, but was
filled with fear and afraid to mention it to anybody. I was
on a straight high for almost five days. Hallucinating like
mad. Oh yes, I was in another dimension—out there in
space.

A pure stroke of luck, I'm sure, saved my life. Since
the age of ten, I had been a surfer. The week when all of
this happened, I decided to go surfing. I wasn't just riding
the waves, I was flying over them. Consequently I was the
victim of a midwave collision with another surfboard and
was knocked out. Hit in the face. I still have a piece of
bone missing from my jaw.

When I came to a lifeguard was hovering over me
and a crowd had gathered. It was all very hazy. That,
however, was my ticket to the hospital. At UCLA Medical
Center I found a very calm atmosphere, which helped me
relax and think. It gave me a chance to do some reevaluat-
ing and I left there with some basic changes. I was more
cautious afterward. I was lucky because I hadn't told my
doctors why all of these strange things were happening to

me. Most attributed my strange behavior to the surfing accident. I was certain others eyed me suspiciously, but nobody ever mentioned drugs. That was a relief. At that time, drugs had a very bad connotation; it was a felony, so I could never have admitted to the doctors that I'd had a bad drug experience.

The reason I'm going into this at such length is to let the kids know it doesn't just end in an afternoon for some people. I had flashbacks for years afterward. Not often, but occasionally. My flashbacks were basically out-of-body experiences that caused me to read up on the subject. That helped me to study myself and lessen the fear I had from the experience. After a time it became a very positive experience—a chance to do a great deal of work on my inner self.

Being the boy as the middle child of three was not as bad as some in-between children find it. I'm close to my two sisters. Jody is the older, Juanita the younger one. We've always had a common ground on which to be united—our parents. Even as children, instead of sibling rivalry, we joined in mutual protest when we thought our parents were unfair.

Our parents never played favorites. Still, they both had their weaknesses. When push came to shove, my father was a hard nut on the surface with a real soft core. He's a sweetheart. Although Mom is a sweetheart externally, she can be tough as nails. They both did their utmost to instill sound principles in their children. Traditions have always been a factor in my family. A man's word is important. Respect and integrity are high on my father's list of priorities, which we were expected to absorb and practice.

Such qualities do not always have an immediate impact. I filed a lot of what my parents said in the back of my mind and proceeded to be what I wanted to be. I was young and had the world by the tail. I broke curfew and sneaked out after everyone else had gone to bed at night. I was not averse to using somebody else's property without permission, as I've already explained. I recall an incident much closer to home. My mother bought Dad a motorcycle. I was an early teen-ager and saw no harm in sneaking it from the garage (when they were out for the evening) and going for a little spin to impress my peers. I'd carefully had a key made from one of Dad's. Making sure I had on a helmet so the cops couldn't tell my age, I'd then take off joyriding with my friends.

The cops, not my parents, caught me. It was three days after I'd received my learner's permit. One night, riding with a friend, I mistakenly forgot the helmet. Always young looking for my age, at that time I could have passed for ten. You can just imagine the officer's reaction when he saw me zipping by on a motorcycle. Not only did I lose my license for six months, but I had to face my father's wrath—and he was incensed. He grounded me for what I considered some God-awful length of time. When he reads this he will no doubt smile at my youthful sense of adventure, but I assure you he wasn't smiling then.

Restrictions were imposed when I broke the rules. My parents were the type of disciplinarians who believed in deprivation of privileges and grounding. I can never remember them beating their children. Oh, we were spanked, but no beatings. There was only one time in my life when my father actually hit me—and I deserved it. I was fourteen and had a big mouth. One evening he was talking to me at the dinner table and I really wasn't interested in whatever sermon he was giving that night, so I more or less told him to kiss off—or words to that effect. Without thinking, his reaction was to strike out at me—and he did. I quickly was aware where the power in the family was coming from. Oh, my God! What a scene for the both

William Katt ☆203

of us. He hurt me more emotionally than physically, but at the time I could only take in the fact that he had actually struck me. He's a very strong man. The true impact hit us both at about the same time and in nothing flat we had our arms around each other. I still remember him crying and swearing he would never hit me again—and he hasn't.

Being from a celebrity family carries some rather natural disadvantages. For instance, I was a terrible student. All the celebrity wealth in the world couldn't change that. I found school extremely boring. It was only after entering college that I began to show any academic smarts. Majoring in music theory with an English minor, my grade averages started to rise; whereas, in junior high and high school, I was lucky to get a passing grade.

My less-than-great attitude could not be blamed on my home life because I did grow up in the same house my parents still live in, had the same parents without the usual Hollywood array of stepparents, and knew I was loved. It just took me longer to develop.

Don't misunderstand me. I didn't grow up in a Hollywood vacuum. Our home was filled with love and understanding, but it was not always totally serene. There is a lot of tension in the entertainment business. Never is that more true than when a husband and wife are both actors, as my parents were. We had pressures that normal families didn't have or wouldn't understand. There were jealousies when one of them was working and the other wasn't. I saw the friction. Kids are not just a speck on the wall. I still carry certain pent-up, deep-seated, hidden feelings that are not necessarily healthy ones.

There were occasions when Mom and Dad would go for months without really being together. Mom would get home late from the studio when she was doing *Perry Mason*. A television series is demanding. She would leave for work early in the morning, as would my father. They crossed paths at breakfast and nudged each other at night when they went to sleep. Sometimes they'd see each other for a couple of hours on Sunday afternoon. There were a lot of "hellos" and "good-byes."

Finally, after nine years on that show, my mother realized she had missed all her children growing up and one day she said, "I'm through with the business for a while. I'm going to be a mother." By that time we were grown and didn't need to be mothered. We were teenagers. I've always hoped my mother understood that it had nothing to do with whether or not I loved her. It was just too late in my life for her to try to go back and pick up the past.

We were cared for pretty much by the live-in maid who was with our family long before I was born. A very wonderful Hungarian lady who assumed the everyday job of raising us. We were lucky. I've heard some horror stories about live-in help in other celebrity households.

There were times when I felt my parents should have divorced many years ago—rather than stay together through all the industry hassles. Sometimes divorce is a healthier solution in spite of love. Yet, they are still together after thirty plus years and still have tremendous love for each other. That speaks for itself. I suppose being such total opposites had something to do with that. Dad grew up in New York's Hell's Kitchen—a tough kid from a tough neighborhood. No family. His father died when he was about two and his mother when he was about sixteen. On the other hand, my mother came from a small town— Rockford, Illinois—proper family environment and all that. Total opposites.

As I've said, I was the rebellious child. Still, traditional things did creep into my life while I was still a teen-ager. For instance, I discovered girls. My first sexual experience was enough to discourage some boys about sex. We were nearly caught by the girl's parents who came home early from an evening out. Talk about going out the second-story window—wow! It was frightening to a young boy to have his first sexual encounter turn into a near disaster. Of course, I can chuckle and see it as a funny incident now.

It is also somewhat funny, or maybe ironic, that I ever got into the motion-picture and television business. As a youngster I didn't evidence the usual signs of thespian talent. Looking back now with an adult's mind I can see the great influences in my life: friends of my parents in the industry, days on the sets, the fact that I used to read scripts and run lines with my parents to help them memorize for the next day's shooting. All of that must surely have left a mark when I was a child.

It was only after viewing the film *Carrie*—seeing myself for the first time up there on the big screen in my first film experience—that I decided seriously to pursue an acting career. I was quite satisfied with myself. Actually, I had appeared in a picture with Anne Baxter and Steve Forrest much earlier. It was something called *The Late Liz*, which was filmed years before I did *Carrie*, and was never released—for which I'm grateful because I was too young to have been able to sustain an acting career of any significance at that time.

My acting career really began away from home during my seventeenth year. I graduated from high school on a Friday. Over the weekend I found a place to live, bought a car, and moved to Newport Beach. On Monday morning I started attending Orange Coast College. Actually my father helped me buy the car. He said, "You find the car you want and I'll match you dollar for dollar." So he paid for half the car. I thought that was pretty neat. Remembering his early environment, my father wanted me to know the value of a dollar. He was never one to fling money around like some Hollywood types. I appreciated that and still do now that I have a family of my own.

At South Coast, in addition to my studies, I found a job assisting with the lighting/sound board at the South Coast Repertoire Theatre. They were performing the West Coast premiere of Joseph Heller's *We Bombed in New Haven*. The play was a very controversial piece for the times, dealing with the pseudointelligence of the establishment and military—implying in strong terms that they were full of crap. I auditioned for the part of young Fisher, got the part, and went on tour. We were performing at Isla Vista, near Santa Barbara, the same week the Bank of America was bombed in 1969. Students nationwide were more or less in a state of rebellion. Consequently the play received a lot of media attention. People in the audience were jumping up and down and applauding. That was the profound seeding of my growth in the direction of acting. *Carrie* brought that seed to full bloom. I'd seen the rushes, but it was nothing like seeing the whole film. What a tremendous difference it was when all the editing and scoring was done and the completed film was projected up there on the big screen.

I can't say my parents didn't help me with my career because they did, opening doors and helping me meet people. They didn't get the jobs for me, however. They took me to the stage door, so to speak, but once it was time for me to go out and perform there was nothing anybody could do to help. Either I performed or I didn't. You either have the magic or you don't. In our business, where it is so expensive today to put something on, friendship isn't enough. It is a business—period.

A family name can be a hindrance, too. When I first started in the business I was Bill Williams, Jr. People tended to regard me as my father's son and not as myself. Nobody wants to be the second anything. I certainly

William Katt ☆ 207

didn't. I wanted to be me, so I changed my name to my father's real name. I said, "William Katt is a fine name and I'll go by that." That helped me jump right out of the box and the next thing I knew I was in *Carrie*. The picture was released and right away everyone was saying I was the next Robert Redford. So I was back in another box. It would seem that anyone who comes from Southern California—the San Fernando Valley in particular—and has blond hair, is the next Robert Redford. I have met Redford once! I enjoy where his head is. He seems to be a caring and involved man.

I'm still young and have a lot of reflecting to do on my life. Some things have profoundly affected my life. The military academy, for instance, and the year I spent in the Air National Guard. I found military service enlightening. It was important to be able to experience firsthand the power among men. What the power is that makes one man superior to another man. Not physical power—but *power*. That can only be experienced in the military. That doesn't mean I didn't curse myself sometimes for being there and cursed everyone around at the time. Still, looking back, it was a valuable experience. Doubly valuable for anybody in this business, where a tremendous amount of self-discipline is required on a daily basis.

In retrospect, as I've said, my parents always loved each other. I think perhaps I would have had them *like* each other more—like who the other person was more—and remember what those reasons were they married for in the first place. That would have made all their children's lives a lot fuller and richer.

You know what else I would have changed? My father has since gone into land and done very well in real estate. I would have had him become involved in film production because he has an incredible mind for the producing end of the business. I don't think my mother should ever have done the *Perry Mason* television series. I would have had her remain in films, because she was getting better and better and had made some terrific pictures. She's a fine actress—and that series just ate her up.

As for myself, I'd like to be smarter. I wish I'd worked on becoming a more cerebral individual, rather than functioning primarily on an emotional basis, which is what I do. Yes, I'm in the right profession for this time around. I'm pleased that my family was more spiritual than religious. It's something I'd like to pass along to my own children.

I don't know that I'd raise my offspring much differently from the way I was raised. Perhaps only in the sense that I'd take into consideration the mistakes that were imposed on me. This entire assessment of my life may be premature—I don't know. Maybe I'm still growing up—at least still growing.